Gift Ideas
for
Elementary Art

Gift Ideas
for
Elementary Art

Jan Easton Kavanagh

The Center for Applied Research in Education, Inc.
521 Fifth Avenue, New York, N.Y. 10017

©1974 by

THE CENTER FOR APPLIED
RESEARCH IN EDUCATION, INC.
NEW YORK

Library of Congress Cataloging in Publication Data

Kavanagh, Jan   E
    Gift ideas for elementary art.

    1. Handicraft. 2. Gifts. I. Title
TT157.K36   745.5   73-13620
ISBN 0-87628-365-2

About the Author

Jan E. Kavanagh received her BA and teaching credential in Art from the University of California, Santa Barbara, and an elementary teaching credential from the University of California, Berkeley. Her experience in art education includes three years as art teacher in a Berkeley elementary school and several years as classroom-art teacher at the kindergarten and third-grade levels in the schools of Albuquerque, New Mexico. Mrs. Kavanagh is presently teaching arts and crafts to both children and adults in Perth, West Australia.

About This Book

In this age of mass production, a gift made by hand becomes a special treasure, particularly if it is made by a loved one. A handmade gift is appealing not only because it is one of a kind, but also because it can be fitted perfectly to the taste and needs of the recipient. And the thought and time that go into such a gift make it as meaningful to the giver as to the person who receives it.

This book provides complete, easy-to-follow directions for scores of imaginative yet highly practical gift ideas. While written primarily for the elementary classroom teacher, it will also serve as a useful tool for art specialists, church school teachers, camp directors, arts and crafts centers, recreation leaders, and women's service organizations.

Many occasions arise during the school year when the idea of making a gift seems appropriate and exciting. By using some of the many ideas in this book, teachers can help students discover the satisfying experience that comes from making a gift.

Each gift idea had to meet the following requirements before it was included in the book:

1. *It is inexpensive to make.* Some gifts cost a little more to make than others since the necessary supplies won't be found in a standard school supply room. However, there are ways to cut down on costs, such as using stores that donate supplies–e.g., lumber companies. Many items can be brought from home and, in some cases, students might contribute a small amount of money for necessary materials.

2. *The instructions are easy to follow.* If the steps for one project become too involved, the idea has been eliminated or modified so that it will be quickly comprehended by a person reading the directions for the first time. Many illustrations are included to help make the gifts easily understood.

3. *Room is left for the imagination.* None of the gifts are meant to turn out exactly alike, so the class should definitely *not* look like a "little assembly line!" Variations can be made on each idea to make it very personal and unique.

4. *Materials are easy to obtain.* Materials can be found in the home, dime store, art and craft shop, or hardware store. In the explanation of some gifts, a suggestion as to where to find a certain item will be mentioned.

5. *It has been tried and proven in a classroom situation.* All of the gifts have been made in an elementary classroom. Some of the gifts would be easier to make if tables were set up in one section of the room so that supplies may be shared.

6. *It is practical.* Gifts that are completely impractical (such as a plastic Clorox bottle bank decorated with glitter) or that leave nothing to the child's imagination (such as cutting up greeting cards to paste on the top of a calendar) have been omitted.

The gift ideas are separated into six categories. They are:

1. Gifts to Hang on the Wall
2. Gifts to Use
3. Gifts to Wear
4. Gifts to Display
5. Paper Gifts
6. Gift Ornaments

Children in third grade and above should be able to manage the techniques for all of the gifts. Those gifts which are a little complicated for kindergarteners, first and second graders are identified by an asterisk in content listings. Of course, the teacher will have to take her own class's ability into account when selecting ideas.

When presenting a gift idea for the first time, encourage children to use the example of the gift *only* for the purpose of seeing how it has been made and not to copy. Help them to understand that the gift they are making is a "part of them," and therefore should not look like a neighbor's or anyone else's.

Please pay special attention to the special notes contained in the directions, as they have been included as a result of working with thousands of children and should prove helpful.

Jan Kavanagh

Contents

II   Gifts to Use *(cont.)*

III   Gifts to Wear

IV   Gifts to Display

Dedicated to all my students
who have made these gifts

I–Gifts to Hang on the Wall

Plaster of Paris Plaque
Clay Creature That Moves*
Sand Casting Wall Plaque
Raised Sun Design*
Weeds and Dried Flowers on Wood
Spice Plaque*
Bean and Seed Collage
Framed Family Portrait
Tiny Batik on Wood
Clay Name Plaque
Clay Wind Chime
Burlap Weaving
Clay Weed Pot
Mexican Yarn Picture
Key Holder
Foil Bas Relief*
Coat of Arms
Felt Picture on Covered Wood
Frame for a Photograph
Ojo de Dios*
Sun Mobile
Fish Mobile
Bird Mobile

* More Difficult—for third grade and above

Plaster of Paris Plaque

Making this plaster of Paris plaque is an ideal creative activity for even the youngest child. Any type of painting looks very effective on the plaque.

MATERIALS

—plaster of Paris
—water
—container and spoon
—straws
—mold for plaster, such as a plastic ice cream container lid
—rawhide or yarn
—tempera paint in various colors
—brush
—spray lacquer

PROCEDURE

1. Mix the plaster of Paris as directed. Pour it into a mold, such as a square ice cream lid. The plaque should be at least ¼" thick. Make two holes at the top of the plaque (all the way through) with a straw, or insert a hairpin or fairly stiff bent wire into the plaque while it is still wet to later use as a hanger.

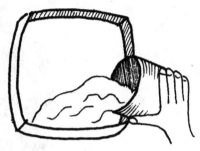

2. Allow the plaster to dry. Then, remove it from the mold.
3. Paint on the smoothest side of the plaster plaque with tempera paints. A totally abstract design works beautifully for this particular gift. Even some splatter painting (flip very wet paint off of the brush onto the plaque) adds to the effect.

4. When the painting has completely dried, spray a lacquer over it to protect it and give it a glossy finish.
5. Thread rawhide or thick yarn through the two holes and tie in a loop for hanging.

VARIATIONS

• Use felt pens to draw on the plaque instead of paint.

Clay Creature that Moves

This clever garden or porch ornament is full of personality and makes a very special gift for anyone.

MATERIALS

—firing clay (preferably red) approximately 4″ diameter ball per child
—kiln
—rolling pin or cylinder to flatten clay
—non-stick surface to work on
—objects to add texture to the clay such as buttons, hairpins, straws, pencils, nails, and screws
—plastic knife
—straw to make holes in clay
—glaze for clay (optional)

PROCEDURE

1. Have each child work on a non-stick surface. Roll out the clay to ¼″ thick all over. (*Note:* Two ¼″ sticks or dowels placed on either side of the rolling pin make this process very simple.)

2. Decide on the design of the animal. Draw it on the flattened clay with a nail. For a first attempt at making this gift, it is easier to make the animal or person in four parts: head, arms, body, and the two legs. Cut the shapes with the knife.

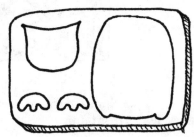

3. Add designs and texture to the shapes with the various objects.

4. Make holes in the clay with the straw. Seven holes are needed for the four-part moving animal or person.

5. Place these four parts on a drying board and keep in a cupboard so they will dry slowly. Turn them over several times in the first day so they will dry flat. A flat object may be placed on top of the clay pieces to prevent warping.

6. After the clay has completely dried, bisque fire the pieces in the kiln.

7. If a glaze is desired, paint it on and fire the clay pieces once again. (*Note:* A shiny finish can be obtained by painting the bisque fired clay with wallpaper glaze, PVA, or Polymer medium.)

8. Attach the separate pieces with rawhide, jute, yarn, or rope. Make a bigger loop at the top for hanging the moving clay animal.

Sand Casting Wall Plaque

A sand casting wall plaque looks very attractive when hanging outside on the patio, or beside the front door.

MATERIALS

—plaster of Paris
—container to mix it in
—old spoon to mix the plaster
—water
—shoe box or other box, one per sand casting
—sand
—sea shells, sticks, and other objects to make designs in the sand
—wire to hang the plaster plaque
—plastic knife
—tooth brush

PROCEDURE

1. Put ½″ of sand in the bottom of a shoe box. Dampen this sand with water so that the imprint of objects pressed into the sand will remain.

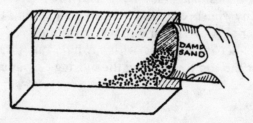

2. Press objects such as shells, sticks, and other items into the dampened sand, making a design with textures. Remove these objects before pouring on the plaster of Paris.

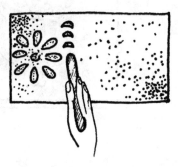

3. Mix up a batch of plaster of Paris. Read the directions on the package carefully and pour quickly into the prepared sand, covering it entirely as evenly as possible and making at least a ½″ thick plaque. Smooth out the back, using a plastic knife. Stick a wire loop into the back to use as a hanger.

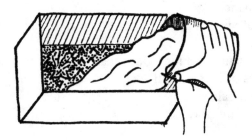

4. When the plaster has dried, tear away the cardboard box and take out the plaque. Brush away the excess sand from the front of the plaque with an old toothbrush so that the design shows through. Don't brush it too clean!

Raised Sun Design

This gift idea should open up the imagination for many more ideas; it's different and effective for all ages.

MATERIALS

—piece of wood (suggested size would be 6" x 8")
—sandpaper
—can of enamel paint and brush (turpentine to clean brush too!)
  or
—spray paint in a high gloss enamel, any color desired
—pieces of colored felt
—cotton balls
—needle and thread
—glue
—scissors
—pop-top lid ring for hanging plaque, and hammer and nail

PROCEDURE

1. Prepare the piece of wood by sanding it, particularly on the corners and edges. Then paint the front and sides of the piece of wood with a shiny enamel paint. Lime green, peacock blue, or red looks good, but any color can be used. Allow the paint to dry.

2. Make the sun. Cut out two circles or ovals from yellow or gold felt. Pin them together and sew around them, leaving a small opening at the bottom for stuffing.

3. Stuff the sun with cotton balls. A pencil works well to distribute the cotton evenly.

4. Sew up the opening, or glue a "chin" at this place, gluing the opening closed at the same time.

5. Add the facial features to the sun—give it a lot of personality!
6. Glue the sun in the middle of the wood.
7. Cut out decorations to go around the sun and arrange them in a pattern encircling it. Glue them to the wood.

8. Nail a pop-top lid ring to the back of the plaque for hanging.

VARIATIONS

• Cover the wood with a solid-colored fabric before gluing on the felt design.
• Make a burlap wall hanging by putting a narrow strip of wood or dowel at each end. Glue the sun design on this.

Weeds and Dried Flowers on Wood

If dried flowers and weeds are readily available, children will enjoy mounting their own arrangements on pieces of prepared wood.

MATERIALS

—an assortment of dried flowers and weeds, as many varieties as possible
—glue
—piece of wood, small, approximately 4″ x 6″
—sandpaper
—stain
—pop-top lid ring for hanging, a nail and hammer
—ribbon bow (optional)

PROCEDURE

1. Prepare the piece of wood by sanding it carefully and rubbing or painting a stain on the front and sides of it.
2. Arrange the bouquet of different dried flowers and weeds on the piece of wood. Place glue on the wood and press the bouquet down gently.
3. A bow may be glued on the bouquet, placed over the stems.
4. Add a pop-top lid ring nailed to the back, for hanging.

VARIATIONS

• Two holes may be drilled in the top of the wood plaque, and leather thonging may be threaded through it and tied in a loop for hanging.

Splice Plaque

Here is a plaque made especially for a kitchen wall!

MATERIALS

—various spices such as:
    fresh ginger
    whole peppercorns
    red chile
    bay leaves
    mustard seeds
    cloves
    garlic (cloves)
    cinnamon sticks
    rosemary
—piece of wood (3" x 9" is an approximate size)
—sandpaper
—glue
—spray lacquer
—black permanent felt pen (type that writes on any surface)
—ring for hanging

PROCEDURE

1. First of all, prepare the piece of wood by sanding it until the edges are

smooth and slightly rounded. The piece of wood may be *any* size, but a narrow one is easiest to arrange the spices on.

2. Decide on the spices to use and arrange them on the wood. Glue them on the wood with enough glue to hold them securely.

3. Using the felt pen, write the names of the spices near them as artistically and interestingly as possible.

4. Arrange the word "spices" somewhere on the display. Add a few simple designs with the felt pen if desired.

5. Spray the entire plaque with the spray lacquer, to protect the spices.

6. Attach a ring at the top for hanging.

VARIATIONS

• Add dried flowers to the plaque for effect.

• Glue the spices on a piece of beige burlap and use as a wall hanging.

• Glue a grosgrain ribbon around the edge of the wooden plaque to give these edges a tidy look.

Bean and Seed Collage

Gather a good variety of seeds and beans for this gift idea. It's unusual and lots of fun!

MATERIALS

—different types of seeds
—different types of beans
—glue
—pencil
—wood block, approximately 4" x 6"
—pop-top can ring for hanging, nail and hammer
—shellac and brush
—sandpaper

PROCEDURE

1. Plan a design that will be feasible to reproduce in a bean and seed collage. A completely abstract design works well, as does a simple object such as a flower or bird.

2. Sketch the design on a sanded block of wood. Apply glue to an area and neatly arrange the beans and seeds on it. Try to put contrasting colors in separate sections to show the various parts of the design.

3. After all the seeds and beans have been glued on, shake the wood block gently to see if there are any loose seeds or beans.

4. Brush shellac or varnish on the entire front of the wood block for added protection.

5. Nail a pop-top lid ring on the back of the wood block for hanging.

VARIATIONS

• Glue the seeds or beans on cardboard instead of wood.

• Add macaroni or twine to the bean and seed collage.

• Cover the entire front of the wood with beans and seeds so that no wood shows.

Framed Family Portrait

A special drawing, such as a family portrait, presented in its own frame, will make a loving and lasting gift—one that's quick and simple to make as well!

MATERIALS

—lid of a shoe box or other available box lid
—white drawing paper (the size of the box lid)
—crayons, colored chalk, charcoal, paint and brush, or felt pens
—tempera paint or poster paint and brush (black paint works well)
—glue
—scissors

PROCEDURES

1. Discuss what a family portrait is and have the children think of how they would draw all the members of their family, including pets.
2. Give each student a piece of white drawing paper. Trace around the box lid with a pencil. This will be the size of paper on which the portrait will be done.
3. Encourage the children to take time with their drawings and pay attention to details. Have them "sign" their drawings upon completion in the bottom right-hand corner.

4. Paint the inside and outside edges of the lid with the tempera paint. Use a large brush and thick paint. Allow this to dry completely.

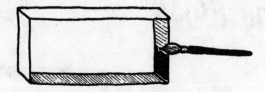

5. After the portrait has been cut out, glue it to the inside of the lid.

VARIATIONS

• Use crayons to draw the portrait. Then, glue this on a piece of wood. After it has dried (under heavy books), brush Polymer medium over the front of the wood.
• Use gold spray paint to paint the cardboard lid frame.
• Clear contact paper can be stuck on top of the portrait to resemble glass.

Tiny Batik on Wood

Some discarded white material, crayons, one color of dye, and a small piece of wood are all that is needed for this gift. It gives the children a chance to use crayons on something other than paper.

MATERIALS

—crayons
—white material (i.e. old sheet)
—one color dye, a dark shade
—container to mix dye in
—tongs or rubber gloves to remove material from dye
—blocks of wood, slightly larger than the piece of white material
—sandpaper (optional)
—glue
—pop-top can lid rings, nail and hammer

PROCEDURE

1. Give children pieces of material, approximately 4″ x 4″ or 4″ x 5″. Have them draw a picture using many colors of crayons (applied heavily)

on this piece of material. Leave some of the material uncolored so the dye will penetrate it.

2. After the crayon has been applied, have the children wad up the small piece of material in their hands so there will be cracks in the crayon.

3. Place the material in the container of dye and remove with tongs or rubber gloves. Allow to dry.

4. If wood is available, it may be sanded before gluing the piece of material to it. A pop-top can ring can be nailed to the back of the wood for hanging.

VARIATIONS

• Glue the piece of material to a piece of colored cardboard, larger than the material.
• Make the little batik into a card, by gluing it on the cover of a piece of folded construction paper.

Clay Name Plaque

Here is a very personal gift that can go near the front door, or serve as an interesting wall hanging anywhere.

MATERIALS

—firing clay, preferably red clay
—kiln in which to fire clay
—glaze to paint on clay (one color will do) optional
—rolling pins (optional)
—objects to add texture to the clay, such as buttons, hairpins, straws, pencils, nails, and screws
—a non-stick surface to work on, such as a piece of burlap
—plastic knife
—straw or nail to make holes in the clay
—rawhide, jute, hemp, twine, or heavy yarn to hang name plaque

PROCEDURE

1. Have each child work on a non-stick surface. Burlap gives the clay a marvelous texture. Give each child a ball of clay, about 2½" in diameter.
2. The clay can be rolled out with a rolling pin, but the palm of the hand could be used instead. Make sure that the clay is at least ¼" thick all over.
3. Use a knife to cut the clay into a plaque shape—rectangular, for instance. The plaque could be oval shaped, square shaped, or any shape.

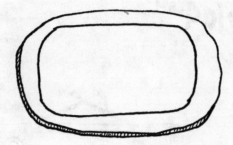

4. Use a nail or other sharp object to draw on the clay, after the plaque has been smoothed. Write the name(s) on the plaque with the nail and add other designs. Make textures in the clay with the various objects. Be sure the name is bold and very visible. Add two holes at the top for hanging.

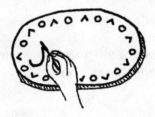

5. Allow to dry thoroughly before firing in the kiln. Dry in a cupboard and turn the plaque over several times, so it dries easily and does not warp.

6. Bisque fire in the kiln.

7. Paint on a glaze and fire once more. Or, rub shoe polish wax over the plaque and rub off with a rag. The plaque could also be painted with P.V.A., Polymer medium, or wallpaper glaze.

8. Thread rawhide through the holes and make a loop, large enough for hanging.

VARIATIONS

• Make the letters of the name or designs on the plaque raised by cutting them out with a knife from bits of clay and sticking them to the smoothed plaque. A "slip" or mixture of clay and water is needed to adhere them.

• Use a nail to dig a few little holes into the plaque to stick dried flowers into later.

Clay Wind Chime

Clay wind chimes are lovely in a garden, hanging on a porch, or even as a decoration inside the home.

MATERIALS

—clay, the firing type
—kiln in which to fire clay
—glaze to paint on clay (optional)
—rolling pins or other cylinders (optional)
—objects to add texture to the clay, such as buttons, hairpins, straws, nails, pencils, and screws
—a non-stick surface to work on
—plastic knife
—straw to make holes in the clay
—rawhide, jute, hemp, twine, or heavy yarn to hang wind chimes

PROCEDURE

1. Give each child a ball of clay, about four inches in diameter. Have

them work on a non-stick surface. Flatten out the clay. A rolling pin may be used but it is not necessary. The palm of the hand can get the clay flat enough for this project.

2. Cut various shapes out of the flattened clay with the knife. Make sure they are all at least ¼" thick. Beads may be made as well.

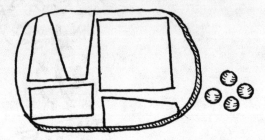

3. Add texture and design to the shapes with the various objects.

4. Make holes in the clay where the rawhide will go, using a straw.

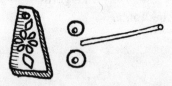

5. Allow to dry slowly. Keep in a cabinet and turn over several times during the first few days.

6. Bisque fire the clay in the kiln.

7. Then add glaze if desired. However, the natural clay looks attractive unglazed for this project. If glaze has been painted on, fire once more in the kiln.

8. Attach the various shapes together, using the rawhide to hang as a wind chime or garden decoration. They can all be hung from the largest shape, or can be hung from a twig, piece of driftwood, or some such object.

VARIATIONS

• Add wooden beads as spacers for the wind chime.
• Rub shoe polish wax on some of the pieces of the wind chime for variation.

Burlap Weaving

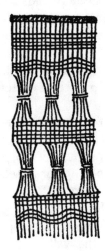

By using a piece of burlap as the basis for a wall hanging, an interesting form of weaving results—a good introduction to real fabric weaving.

MATERIALS

—burlap, approximately 12″ x 18″ per person—colored or natural
—scissors
—yarn and other strings
—wide-eyed needles
—dowel, rod, or stick as wide as the wall hanging
—weeds or dried flowers (optional)

PROCEDURE

Interesting designs can be made by pulling some of the threads from a piece of burlap. The remaining threads can be rearranged in a variety of ways to enhance the design.

Here are some ways of creating an interesting design.

1. Pull some threads to leave an open weave.
2. Pull alternate strands to make a loose weave.
3. Move parts of the remaining strands up and down to form curved lines.
4. Pull threads in both directions to create open spaces.
5. Group threads going down together and tie in groups to form spaces.
6. Weave other threads through threads going down where threads going across have been removed.
7. Weave sticks, weeds, or dried flowers into open spaces.
8. Make fringe or tassels with strands pulled from the burlap.
9. Exchange different colors of strands removed from the burlap with other students.
10. To finish, hem top edge. Slip a dowel, rod, or stick through and hang on the wall.

Clay Weed Pot

These little clay weed or straw flower pots are easy enough for pre-schoolers to make and are very quaint and appealing additions to any wall.

MATERIALS

—firing clay (preferably red clay)
—kiln in which to fire clay
—glaze to paint on clay (one color will do) optional
—rolling pins (optional)
—objects to add texture to the clay, such as buttons, hairpins, straws, pencils, nails, and screws
—a non-stick surface to work on, such as a piece of burlap
—tissue to stuff in pocket of clay
—plastic knife
—straw or nail to make holes in the clay
—rawhide, jute, hemp, twine, or heavy yarn to hang pot

PROCEDURE

1. Have each child work on a non-stick surface. Burlap gives the clay a marvelous texture. Give each child a ball of clay, about 2″ in diameter.
2. The clay can be rolled out with a rolling pin, but the palm of the hand could be used instead. Make sure that the clay is at least ¼″ thick all over.
3. Use a knife to cut off the four rounded sides to make a rectangle.

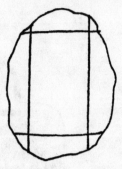

4. Fold up part of the rectangle to form a "pocket" as shown. Pinch the edges together gently, making sure they are securely stuck together.

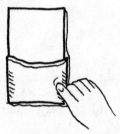

5. Make two holes with a straw at the top of the weed pot for hanging.
6. Add texture and a design to the clay with various objects.

7. Stick a tissue in the pocket to make it stand away from the back of the pot. Remove this when the clay has hardened. Dry in a cupboard slowly and turn the pots over several times in the first days of drying.

8. Bisque fire the pot. This is the first firing in the kiln.
9. Paint on the glaze. Leave some of the clay unglazed for a rustic effect.
10. Fire once again in the kiln.
11. Find some pretty weeds and mix with tiny straw flowers to fill the pocket and make the gift complete.
12. String the rawhide through the holes and tie in a knot.

VARIATIONS

• Leave the weed pot as "bisque ware" (fired in the kiln once) instead of adding a glaze.
• Paint tempera paints or watercolors on part of the weed pot. Then brush PVA or Polymer medium over the entire weed pot.

Mexican Yarn Picture

Making Mexican yarn pictures is fun and easy for children of all ages.

MATERIALS

—6″ x 9″ or 9″ x 12″ piece of tagboard, chipboard, or cardboard
—many different colors of yarn, string, and roving (very wide yarn)
—white glue
—scissors
—pencil
—newspaper to work on

PROCEDURE

1. Using a pencil, draw the outline of a picture on the cardboard. Make it simple and large.

2. Place white glue along the lines of the picture and press the yarn on top of the glue.

3. Put glue inside the shapes of the design and fill it in completely with yarn. Fill in the background with a plain color of yarn. Work carefully so that the finished project is neat. Check that all ends of yarn are glued down.

(*Note:* Have children gather yarn from home and distribute it before beginning to glue.)

VARIATIONS

- Use felt along with the yarn.
- Work on a piece of fabric instead of cardboard, and leave some of the fabric exposed. The fabric may be glued to a piece of cardboard.

Key Holder

Here is a useful gift that requires a new technique for some (hammering nails!).

MATERIALS

—piece of wood (approximately 4″ x 6″ and 3/4″ thick)
   (*Note:* Usually, scraps such as this are in the trash bin at lumber stores.)
—newspaper or newsprint
—tissue paper in various colors
—diluted white glue (one part water to one part glue) or liquid starch and container
—permanent felt pen in a dark color

PROCEDURE

1. Each person should have the following: a piece of wood, newspaper (or newsprint), tissue paper, and diluted glue.
2. Begin by tearing the newspaper into small irregular pieces, no larger than 1″ x 1″. Do likewise with the tissue paper. (*Note:* Several different colors of tissue paper could be used. Good color combinations are: hot pink, orange, and red; green, turquoise, and chartreuse.)
3. Dip the newspaper pieces into the glue mixture or liquid starch (even wheat paste will work for this step, but not when applying the tissue paper). Apply them to the piece of wood, covering the sides as well. Bring the newspaper pieces on the edges around to the back side of the wood as well.

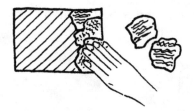  

4. Repeat the exact procedure using the tissue paper. (*Note:* If the print from the newspaper has rubbed off on the students' fingers, they should be washed before handling the tissue paper.) Allow to dry completely.

5. Use a permanent felt pen to write KEYS on the collage. Several types of lettering could be written on the chalkboard to serve as examples.

6. To add nails: evenly space the nails along the bottom of the wood, making sure that each is perpendicular to the wood and hammered in deeply enough to be firm.

7. To add hooks: Evenly space the hooks under the bottom edge of the wood and mark where they will be placed. Use a nail to hammer holes

into the wood, being careful to make them straight. Screw the hooks into the holes until they are tight.

8. This key holder can be put on the wall by hammering one long nail through it and into the wall, or by attaching two pop-top can rings to the back (so the key holder is stable).

VARIATIONS

• Use enamel paint to paint the sanded wood. Add felt decorations and cut the word *KEYS* out of felt as well.

Foil Bas Relief

A three-dimensional foil bas relief makes an interesting item to display on any wall.

MATERIALS

—cardboard (one piece for the base and more for cutting out shapes)
—string or cord (optional)
—glue
—scissors
—aluminum foil (preferably "heavy duty")
—steel wool
—spray paint or India ink

PROCEDURE

1.   Sketch a design on the large piece of cardboard. Split the design into smaller, composite sections.

2.   Cut out cardboard shapes to fit the sections of the design.

3.   Glue these pieces into place on the base piece of cardboard.

4.   The design can be built up by adding smaller pieces of cardboard on top of those already glued.
5.   String or cord can be glued down to carry out the design.
6.   Cut a piece of aluminum foil, large enough to cover the base cardboard, with several inches to spare. Crumple the aluminum foil.

7.   Apply glue to the front side of the cardboard design, making sure to cover every hollow.
8.   Center the aluminum foil over the design and press down in the center. Carefully smooth the foil over the raised sections and into the hollows, working from the center outwards. Then, smooth over each edge. The design will stand out as a raised relief pattern. Use a pencil to draw on the foil, bringing out the design and adding texture.

9.   Turn the cardboard over, fold the aluminum foil around the edges, and glue.

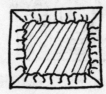

10. Spray paint the front of the relief (preferably outside, on newspaper) or paint with India ink. Matt Black spray paint is effective, but other colors could be used as well. Allow to dry.

11. Carefully rub some of the paint off the raised sections with fine steel wool. Work slowly and gently or the foil may tear. Continue rubbing until all the raised sections are clearly exposed. (*Note:* If the aluminum foil does tear, respray the area with paint.)

VARIATIONS

• Make a small relief picture as described, then glue it onto a sanded, stained piece of wood.
• Use white glue to "draw" a raised picture or design on the cardboard. When the glue becomes hard, cover the cardboard with aluminum foil and continue as described above.

Coat of Arms

Here is a fun little gift and a small history lesson as well! Make sure the children understand what a coat of arms is before beginning to work. Coats of arms were family emblems first used to identify every family.

MATERIALS

—paper
—pencil
—cardboard
—pattern (optional)
—aluminum foil, the heaviest available
—construction paper, same size as the cardboard
—glue
—scissors
—Italic Alphabet chart (as shown)

PROCEDURE

1. Try to show the students examples of coats of arms and heraldic designs. There should be some good examples in books on knights, castles, and feudal life. After they have viewed some actual coat of arms designs, tell them to draw a coat of arms for themselves. Plan it on paper first. Use the pattern as an outline.

2. Cut the coat of arms shape out of cardboard. Cover this shape with foil. Bend it around the edges and onto the back of the shape.

3. Transfer the coat of arms design from the paper to the foil by placing the paper over the foil and drawing over the design with a pencil. Press down hard so that the design is transferred to the foil.

4. Remove the paper and continue working directly on the foil with the pencil. Create various textures with lines and designs. Vary the width of the lines as well.

5. Cut a piece of construction paper slightly smaller than the coat of arms shape. Then, place glue all over the back of the coat of arms. Carefully press the construction paper shape over the back of the coat of arms. Place several heavy books on top of this until the glue has dried.

ABCDEFGHIJKL
MNOPQRSTUVWXYZ

VARIATIONS

• Finish the coat of arms with black ink as described in the gift idea, "Foil Bas Relief" on page 47.
• Put felt on the back of the coat of arms instead of construction paper.
• Build up the design with cardboard shapes (glued to the cardboard coat of arm shape) as described in the gift idea, "Foil Bas Relief" on page 47.

Felt Picture on Covered Wood

This little fabric and felt wall plaque is a sweet gift to be displayed anywhere.

MATERIALS

—colored felt
—fabric in small prints, checked, or striped for background
—glue
—scissors (sharp enough to cut felt)
—yarn
—black sequins
—rickrack, trim, braid, lace, buttons, bits of fabric, etc.
—toothpick for applying glue
—small piece of wood, approximately 4" x 6" (cardboard could be substituted)
—ring for hanging, or pop-top lid ring and nail

PROCEDURE

1. Decide on a design for the little plaque, something that will be interesting when made into a felt collage.
2. Cover the piece of wood with a piece of fabric. Use a piece of fabric that is about two inches wider and longer than the wood and pull it tightly over all four sides of the wood. Glue down with glue placed on the back of the wood. A piece of felt could be placed over the back to make it look finished.

3. Cut out the parts of the design from felt and arrange them on the covered wood. Add accessories using the various items listed in *Materials.* Sequins are good for eyes, and yarn works well for hair. Don't glue anything down until the design has been arranged on the background in a pleasing way. Children and animals are effective for this gift idea. It is fun when the students make a little full portrait of themselves on the covered wood!

4. To hang the plaque: Use a ring screwed into the top of the wood, or a pop-top can ring nailed to the back of the plaque.

VARIATIONS

- Cover the wood or cardboard with burlap before beginning.
- Do not cover the wood, but glue the felt design directly on the wood.
- Sand the wood, and then paint with a bright enamel.

Frame for a Photograph

Here's a gift that is particularly fun if the teacher or some volunteer can take a snapshot of each child (one that his parents haven't seen) to put in this extremely personal little frame!

MATERIALS

—cardboard
—scissors
—newsprint
—tissue paper in various colors
—liquid starch
—cord
—glue
—photograph of child
—Polymer medium, P.V.A., or wallpaper glaze and brush

PROCEDURE

1. Trace the shape of the photograph on a piece of cardboard. Then, make a one-inch margin around this shape. This will be the size of the frame. Make another line, ¼" in from the photograph shape. The edges may be rounded.

2. Cut out the cardboard frame.

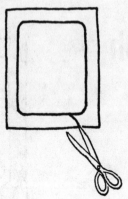

3. Tear a piece of newsprint into small pieces. Dip them into liquid starch and apply them to front, back, and edges of the cardboard frame. Allow it to dry, making sure it doesn't warp. A flat, heavy object may be needed to keep it flat.

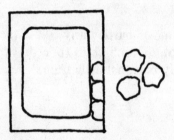

4. Arrange pieces of cord around the border of the frame. When this design is satisfying, glue it down and let dry completely.

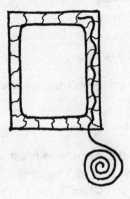

5. Dip small pieces of colored tissue paper into liquid starch and apply over the newsprint and cord design, covering the frame completely. (*Note:* Good tissue paper color combinations: yellow-orange-red; turquoise-green-blue; hot pink-orange.) Allow this to dry.

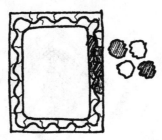

6. Brush Polymer medium on the front of the frame, to shine it and protect it.

7. Make the back using another piece of cardboard. Cut out a flap as shown to allow the frame to stand up. Tape the child's photograph behind the frame. Then, using either glue or tape, attach the back of the frame to the front of the frame to complete the gift.

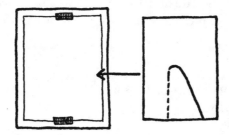

VARIATIONS

• Omit the cord and use a single, light shade of tissue paper collage over the newsprint. Then, with felt pens, draw a design around the border of the frame.

• Place a neatly printed poem the student has created (instead of the photograph) inside the frame.

Ojos de Dios

An Ojo (oh-ho) de Dios or Eye of God is a type of Paho, a prayer offering used by the Hiuchol Indians of Mexico to convey goodness and obliterate evil. It expresses wishes for good health, fortune and long life.

MATERIALS

—two sticks per ojo (dowels, popsicle sticks, toothpicks, etc.)
—various colors of yarn
—glue
—scissors

PROCEDURE

1. Cross the sticks. Pre-gluing or wiring may make them easier to handle.

2. Tie a piece of yarn at the intersection and start winding each arm consecutively. Go over and around each stick, keeping the yarn fairly tight. Work counterclockwise (unless left-handed). (*Note:* To prevent

slipping, put a thin line of white glue on the sticks before they are wrapped. Wind over the wet glue.)

3. To change color, merely knot the new yarn so that the knot falls on the back side of the ojo. To create spaces between the strands of yarn, go around each stick two or three times before going to the next one. The various shapes are determined by the number of windings around each stick.

4. Pompons can be tied at the tips of the cross pieces. Pompons are made by wrapping yarn around a piece of cardboard that is cut to the size of the desired pompon. Gather and tie the yarn at one end of the cardboard and cut the yarn at the opposite end. Remove the cardboard. Hold the strands of the pompon in one hand with the gathered section exposed. Wrap with yarn a short distance from the top (as shown).

Sun Mobile

This sun mobile is one of the simplest types of mobiles, yet a lovely gift for any member of a family.

MATERIALS

—9″ x 9″ square of yellow paper, preferably tagboard or thin cardboard
—scissors
—pencil
—needle and thread (invisible thread works well)
—felt pen (possibly orange ink) optional

PROCEDURE

1. Draw a circle on the yellow paper, to the edge of the paper. (*Note: Patterns or round objects, such as plates, may be used here.*) Draw a smaller circle in the middle.
2. Draw a pattern around the outside edge of the circle to be the sun's "rays." This can be any design the child desires. It may be helpful to show examples.

3. Cut out the design and the circle inside the design. Then, make the inside circle a little smaller so it will swing easily in the middle.

4. Sew the small circle into the middle of the sun's "rays" at one point. Leave some string to hang the sun from the ceiling.

5. Decorate the mobile or write something on it with the felt pen.

VARIATIONS

• Use several colors of tagboard—one for the inside and one for the outside of the sun, or glue two colors back to back.

• Make three or four smaller suns in the same way and hang them, one on top of another, from the ceiling.

Fish Mobile

If reed, used in weaving baskets, can be found, this is an effective and fun mobile to make.

MATERIALS

—reed
—tissue paper in various colors
—scissors
—glue
—toothpick for applying glue
—newspaper to work on
—cellophane tape or very thin wire for fastening reed shape
—thread and needle (preferably invisible thread)

PROCEDURE

1. Cut reed to desired sizes. Form the fish shape by bending the reed and fastening the ends with cellophane tape or thin wire.

2. Place the reed shape on a piece of newspaper. Put a thin line of glue on the face up side of the reed. Place a piece of colored tissue paper, slightly larger than the shape, over this. Press gently and allow to dry.

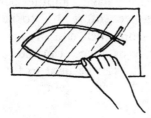

3. Turn the reed shape over and glue a piece of tissue paper to this side in the same manner. Allow to dry.

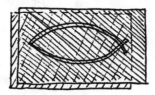

4. Cut around the reed shape carefully, a fraction of an inch away from the reed.

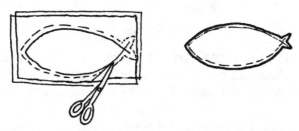

5. Cut features out of other colors of tissue paper, such as fins, tails, scales, and eyes. Glue these onto the fish shape (both sides) with a tiny amount of glue applied with the toothpick.

6. Make as many fish as desired for the mobile. Use several pieces of reed to make the mobile. Attach a thread to the top of each fish with a needle. Tie off neatly.

7. Mobiles can be hung in several different ways, but they all need to be hung while balancing the shapes. This can be done by suspending the rods on which they are to hang from the top of a doorway, on a string between the backs of two chairs, or by having another person hold it.

(a) If one simple cross-piece of reed is to be used, start by balancing shapes hung by thread from each end of one cross-piece. Once this has been done, the other cross-piece can be similarly balanced. When everything is balanced, glue can be used to fix the thread to the reed to stop it from slipping out of balance again.

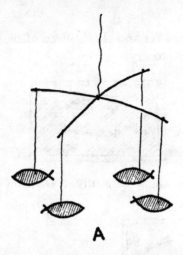

A

(b) Another method of suspension is to balance two shapes on a piece of reed. Find the balancing point of this and, with another thread, suspend it from another piece of reed and balance this with another shape or pair of shapes.

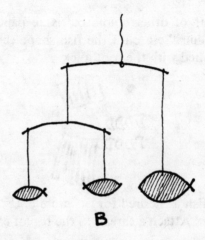

B

VARIATIONS

• Make abstract shapes by bending the reed in various places and cover them with tissue paper.

• Make flowers by bending the reed into circles which will be the centers of the flowers. Glue tissue paper petals around these circles.

Bird Mobile

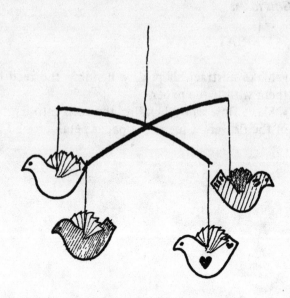

This paper mobile is extremely simple to make and can be varied in a number of ways to make each mobile different.

MATERIALS

—colored construction paper
—colored tissue paper, four 4" x 3" pieces
—felt pens
—needle and thread
—scissors
—wire or sticks for constructing the mobile (reed, bamboo, thin dowels, straws)
—pencil

PROCEDURE

1. Decide which colors to use to make the birds' bodies (construction paper) and wings (tissue paper). Use the pattern (or design another bird shape) to trace four bird bodies.

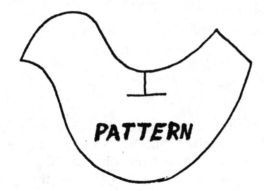

2. Cut out the bodies and cut the paper along the "T." This is where the wings will later be inserted.

3. Use felt pens to make the beak, eyes, and any designs on the body. (Or, cut them out of colored paper.)

4. Fold four pieces of tissue paper accordian style in ¼" folds.

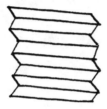

5. Slip this folded piece of tissue paper through the slit in the bird, half way. Repeat for the other three birds.

6. Spread out the folds to form a fan. Fasten the two ends that come together with the needle and thread. Leave a foot of thread to tie on the sticks.

7. To construct the mobile: *See* directions for balancing a mobile in the *Fish Mobile Gift Idea* (#7 in *Procedures*) on page 62.

VARIATIONS

• Use colored tagboard for the body and origami paper for the wings.
• A beautiful Christmas mobile would be to make the four birds white doves, using white construction paper and white tissue paper. Use orange felt pen for the beak and a black felt pen to draw the eyes. An olive branch could be made out of green tissue paper and glued to the beak.
• Make two birds and attach to each end of a stick. Tie a thread in the middle for hanging.

Note: The smallest-sized stapler could be used to attach the thread to the wings when fastening them together.

II—Gifts to Use

Clay Hot Plates
Sachet
Pin Cushion
Burlap Bulletin Board*
Decorated Cigar Box*
Pot Holder
Clay Paper Weight
Key Chain
Magnetic Note Holder
Candle Holder
Decorated Notebook
Bean Bag
Sunglass Case
Recipe Holder
Clay and Gravel Paper Weight*
Papier Mache Napkin Rings
Clay Napkin Rings
Felt Bookmark
Plant in Homemade Pot
Letter Rack
Papier Mache Piggy Bank*

* More Difficult—for third grade and above

Clay Hot Plates

A clay hot plate is not only a practical gift, but one that can be treasured forever—and it could also serve as a wall plaque!

MATERIALS

—firing clay
—kiln in which to fire clay
—two dowels, rulers, or sticks of the same thickness
—rolling pin, bottle, jar, etc. to roll clay
—objects to make textures in clay such as nails, toothpicks, screws, buttons, etc.
—a 5" or 6" square cardboard pattern
—glazes to paint on clay, and brushes
—felt piece, the size of the pattern
—glue
—scissors
—non-stick surface to work on

PROCEDURE

1. Give each student a ball of clay and have them work with it until all the air bubbles are removed. Place the clay between the two dowels. Roll it out with a rolling pin, using the two dowels as guides to keep the clay the same thickness all over. Make the clay at least ¼" thick and larger than the cardboard pattern.

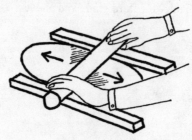

2. Place the pattern on top of the rolled out clay and cut out a square of clay, using a knife and following the edge of the pattern carefully. Have students put initials on the back of the clay.

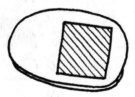

3. Draw a design on the clay square using various objects.

4. Dry the clay slowly in a cupboard, putting a weight on top of the clay and turning it over several times so that it will not warp.
5. Fire the clay after it has thoroughly dried.
6. Put a glaze on the face of the hot plate and fire once again.
7. Cut out a piece of felt the size of the hot plate, and glue it to the bottom of the clay.

VARIATIONS

• Put two holes with a straw through the top of the clay square and put leather thonging through it to hang as a wall plaque.
• Do not glaze the clay, but rub shoe polish wax into the clay designs.

Sachet

There are many ways to make a sachet and it's such a lovely gift to give.

MATERIALS

—sachet powder or dried rose petals
—pieces of colored felt
—sequins, ribbon, lace, yarn
—needle and thread
—glue
—scissors, sharp enough to cut through felt
—cotton

PROCEDURE

1. Decide upon the design of the sachet. (Examples: bird, butterfly, apple, flower, heart.) Cut out two pieces of the outline of the design from the felt.

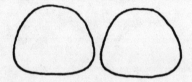

2. When these two main pieces have been cut out, place one piece on top of the other and sew neatly around them with the needle and thread, leaving a small opening for stuffing.

3. Add other pieces of colored felt to the main design. Either glue them on or sew them on. Sequins can be glued or sewn on for a glittery effect. Yarn and/or ribbons can be added.

4. Pour some sachet powder on some cotton and stuff it through the small opening in the sachet. If rose petals (dried and crushed) are used, stuff them through the opening as well.

5. Sew up the opening with the needle and thread.

VARIATIONS

• Use tiny printed fabric instead of felt. Use pinking shears instead of regular scissors.

Pin Cushion

This cute, little hat pin cushion can be placed on a shelf, or hung on the wall. Either way, it will be attractive and useful.

MATERIALS

—2″ styrofoam ball, cut in half with a knife
—felt (for making rim of hat, and small scraps for making flowers)
—scissors, sharp enough to cut through felt
—ribbon or rickrack
—glue
—fabric for wrapping over styrofoam ball
—sequins, buttons, lace (optional) for adding decorations

PROCEDURE

1. One styrofoam ball will make two hat pin cushions. With a knife, cut through the center of the styrofoam ball. Cover this with a square of fabric; the thinner the fabric, the easier this will be to do. Glue or pin this fabric to the bottom of the half-circle.

2. Cut out the rim of the hat from felt. A circle pattern, several inches larger than the ball, could be used.

3. Glue the half-circle to the center of this circle of felt and allow to dry.

4. Put a ribbon, lace, or rickrack band around the hat.

5. Add flowers or other decorations to the band of the hat.

VARIATIONS

• Use foam rubber, old nylon stockings, or cotton to make the rounded part of the hat, instead of styrofoam.

Burlap Bulletin Board

Bulletin boards make a challenging project and are practical gifts to decorate a kitchen or any wall.

MATERIALS

—six pieces of newspaper
—piece of cardboard, the size of the bulletin board
—burlap or other material to cover bulletin board
—masking tape
—felt scraps
—scissors, sharp enough to cut through felt
—glue
—yarn or rickrack (optional)
—pins or tacks and paper to write notes on (optional)

PROCEDURE

1. Place the piece of cardboard in the middle of a stack of at least six newspapers (to pad the board).

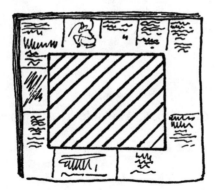

2. Fold these newspapers around the cardboard and tape down with masking tape.

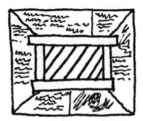

3. Do the same with.a piece of burlap, making sure it is large enough to cover the newspaper.

4. Decorate the front of the bulletin board with designs cut out of felt. Appropriate words could be cut out of the felt. Glue them carefully to the burlap. Rickrack and/or yarn may be glued down as well.

5. Funny notes could be added to the bulletin board before presenting it as a gift.

VARIATIONS

• Use real bulletin board wood, available at a lumber store, instead of newspaper-padded cardboard.

Decorated Cigar Box

A sturdy decorated cigar box can be used for storing many things. It's a useful as well as artistic object d'art.

MATERIALS

—cigar box, one per student
—newspaper or newsprint to cover box
—construction paper, to cover inside lid
—tissue paper in various colors
—liquid starch and container
—Polymer medium, PVA, or wallpaper glaze, and brush
—origami paper
—glue
—scissors
—piece of felt to glue on the bottom of the box (optional)

PROCEDURE

1. A layer of torn pieces of newspaper or plain newsprint is first applied to the lids and sides of the cigar box. Liquid starch (or wheat paste) can be used to accomplish this. (*Note:* This layer's purpose is to cover up the writing on the cigar box. The newspaper print will show through the tissue paper layer for an interesting effect. Using plain newsprint will make the tissue paper colors more predominant.)

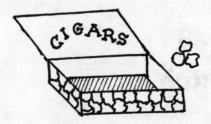

2. After the layer of newspaper or newsprint has been applied, tear small pieces of tissue paper (several colors that blend nicely together or just one shade) and apply them with liquid starch on the top of the lid and the sides of the box. Allow these layers to dry.

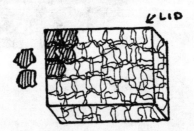

3. Add decorations, cut or torn out of origami paper and glued on over the tissue paper collage. (*Note:* The designs could be cut or torn out of darker pieces of tissue paper instead.)

4. Cut a piece of construction paper the size of the lid and glue it to the inside.
5. Brush Polymer medium over the top and sides of the cigar box to protect it and give it a glossy finish. Leave the lid open until the box is completely dry.
6. Cut a piece of felt to fit the bottom of the cigar box and glue it down.

VARIATIONS

• Cover the cigar box with felt instead of tissue paper.

Pot Holder

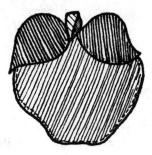

This colorful pot holder can be used as a decorative object to hang on the wall as well as to handle hot pots.

MATERIALS

—old mattress pad or something to pad the pot holder
—felt (or fabric) to make pot holder
—needle and thread
—scissors
—straight pins

PROCEDURE

1. Decide on the basic shape of the pot holder. It could be a slice of watermelon, a pear, apple, or orange. It could also be a stylized flower, heart, or any other design. Cut two of these basic shapes out of the felt (or fabric, as this would make the gift less expensive). Then, cut the same shape, ¼" smaller, out of the mattress pad.

2. Place the mattress pad shape between the two pieces of felt and pin the three pieces together. (*Note:* If fabric that ravels is used, the two pieces of fabric will first have to be sewn on the wrong side, turned inside out, and

the padding will have to be inserted through an opening which will later be sewn together.)

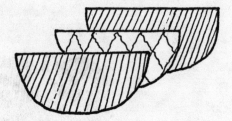

3. Sew around the shapes with a needle and thread. Add a little loop of felt to use in hanging the pot holder.
4. Cut out additional shapes to sew to the pot holder for decoration, such as leaves for the pear or apple. Sew these on neatly.

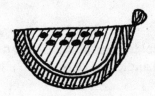

VARIATIONS

• Make a "mitten" type pot holder in the same way, making everything double.
• Stick a small magnet inside the pot holder before sewing it up so the pot holder will stick to the stove and refrigerator and will not need the felt strip loop for hanging.
• Sew a metal or plastic curtain ring to the potholder for hanging.

Clay Paper Weight

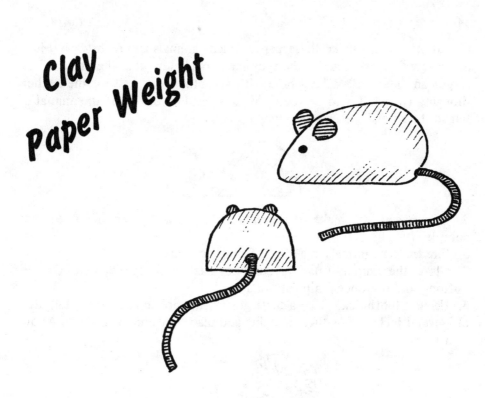

A clay paper weight like the one described will be fun to use as a shelf decoration as well.

MATERIALS

—firing or self-hardening clay
—kiln (in which to fire clay)
—objects for working with clay, such as nail, toothpick, screw, and garlic press or strainer (for making "hair")
—small amounts of felt to glue to bottom (optional)
—leather thonging for "tail"
—glue
—glaze to paint on clay (optional)
—scissors

PROCEDURE

1. Give each child a 1½" ball of clay. Demonstrate how to make the simplest animal that is sitting down, so no legs or arms are necessary. Work with the clay at first so there are no air bubbles left in it. Tell them

not to attempt to make these paper weight animals too realistic, but just add a few features, such as the eyes and ears to show that the little ball of clay is an "animal." Make a hole with a toothpick or nail for the leather thonging (if a tail is to be used). Make sure the bottom of the animal is flat so the animal sits up securely.

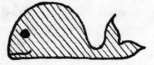

2. Use fingers to make the animal smooth and then allow to dry completely.

3. Fire the clay animals in a kiln if firing clay is used.

4. Glaze the animal (making sure no glaze has been painted on the bottom) and fire once again (optional).

5. Using a toothpick, place a little glue in the hole made for the tail. Cut off several inches of leather thonging and place one end in the hole. Allow to dry.

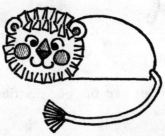

6. Trace around the bottom of the animal on felt and cut this shape out. Glue the felt to the bottom of the animal to complete it.

VARIATIONS

• Shine the unglazed animal with wallpaper glaze, PVA, or Polymer medium.

Key Chain

A key ring and a small piece of wood with a hole drilled through one corner of it is necessary to make this gift.

MATERIALS
—small chain to put keys on
   or
—key chain (they sell in hobby or lapidary shops for around 15¢ and small ring for attaching it to wood.
—piece of wood (approximately 1½" x 2½", or 2½" x 2½") with hole drilled through one corner
—sandpaper
—shellac and brush (and turpentine to clean brush)
—acrylic or enamel paints and tiny brushes

PROCEDURE

1. Carefully sand the edges and corners of the small piece of wood.
2. Decide on a small design or drawing before beginning to paint. This design can be drawn on a piece of paper.
3. Paint the design on one side of the wood. The name of the person to whom the key chain will be given may be painted on the wood. Some suggestions for designs are: sun, strawberry, mouse, flowers, owl, or bird.
4. When the paint has entirely dried, brush a coat of shellac over the piece

of wood. When this front side has dried, the back may also be painted with shellac.

5. Insert the small chain through the hole in the wood. Or, insert a little ring through the wood and attach the key ring to this.

6. As an added decoration, colored tagboard keys may be placed on the key ring.

VARIATIONS

- Use indelible felt pens to draw the design instead of paint.
- Paint the small piece of wood with a bright enamel paint first.

Magnetic Note Holder

If very thin magnets (or magnet tape) are available, this is a very good gift for decorating a refrigerator door, and for holding notes as well.

MATERIALS

—magnets or magnet tape to glue to the back of the felt decorations
—various colors of felt
—scissors, sharp enough to cut felt
—sequins (optional)
—glue

PROCEDURE

1. Decide on the designs for the little note holders. Then, cut the main shape (i.e. mushrooms, butterflies, flowers) out of felt. (*Note:* If the felt is rather thin, two thicknesses could be used to give the shape strength.)
2. Glue other designs cut out of pieces of colored felt to these main shapes. Sequins could be glued on for accents.
3. Glue the small magnet to the back of the felt shape. A set of four note holders is a nice gift.

VARIATIONS

- Sew the various pieces of felt to the main shape instead of gluing.
- Make two of the main shape, sew them together and stuff the shape with a tiny amount of cotton to make the note holder padded.

Candle Holder

Candle holders can be made in many ways, and it is hoped that this particular way may be the stimulus for many other variations. The completed gift will be especially nice if a candle is placed in it.

MATERIALS

—metal lid, such as a cottage cheese lid (or some shallow lid that gold spray paint will stick to).
—styrofoam (small square to stick the candle in)
—macaroni in various shapes
—gold spray paint
—gold glitter
—nuts (optional)
—glue
—newspaper to work on

PROCEDURE

1. Glue the square of styrofoam in the middle of the shallow lid. This styrofoam will later be used to hold the candle.

2. Glue the pieces of macaroni and nuts around the styrofoam and onto the lid to cover up the sides of the styrofoam. Allow all the glue to dry thoroughly.

3. Spray paint the entire candle holder with gold paint and then sprinkle gold glitter over this to give the holder an extra sparkle.
4. Press a little candle into the styrofoam before presenting it as a gift.

VARIATIONS

• Put a crisp red or green ribbon on the candle holder.
• Make a short cardboard tube and glue to the base of the candle holder (lid) to hold the candle instead of using the styrofoam.

Decorated Notebook

Someone has to provide the little spiral notebook to begin this gift idea, but it is a practical one and fun to make for children of all ages.

MATERIALS

—spiral notebook (any size)
—clear contact paper to cover the decorated cover (about 50¢ a yard)
—construction paper (the size of the notebook cover)
—glue
—scissors
—felt pens
—colorful paper, such as origami paper

PROCEDURE

1. Only the front of the notebook has to be decorated. To begin this, cover the front of the notebook with a piece of construction paper. Trace the outline of the notebook cover on the construction paper. Cut around this, making the paper slightly larger than the notebook paper. Place glue all over the notebook cover and press the construction paper down on the cover. Smooth out any wrinkles and press under several heavy books until the cover has thoroughly dried, so it won't warp. Now, trim around the cover, cutting off the edges of construction paper.

2. Next comes the decorating of the special notebook cover. Words can be cut out of origami paper if the notebook is meant for a certain purpose or for a certain person. Shapes can be cut out as well. Arrange these shapes as attractively as possible on the cover and carefully glue them down, using just a dot of glue.

3. Felt pens can be used to accent some shapes or write words on the cover.

4. Cover the front of the notebook cover with clear contact paper to protect it and give it a finished appearance. (*Note:* The teacher could do this step for the younger students, as it can be a little tricky.)

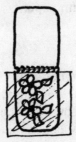

VARIATIONS

• Use a student's favorite crayon or felt pen drawing as the cover.

Bean Bags

Bean bags are a fun gift because they can be used for display purposes, as a doorstop, and anything else the receiver thinks of!

MATERIALS

—dried beans, split peas, or barley for stuffing the bean bags
—scissors, sharp enough for cutting felt
—fabric or felt to make the bean bag case
—yarn and buttons (optional)
—needle and thread or sewing machine
—straight pins
—glue
—paper and pencil

PROCEDURE

1. Decide what shape the bean bag will be and make a pattern out of the piece of paper.
2. Transfer this shape onto the felt or fabric and cut two shapes to sew together for the bean bag case. Cut them out and pin the two shapes together (if they are fabric, pin them inside out).

3. Sew these pieces of fabric or felt together, leaving a small opening in which to insert the beans.

FOR STUFFING

4. Decorate the bean bag to give it a real "personality" with different pieces of felt and possibly yarn or buttons. Glue or sew on these decorations. If glue is used, allow these decorations to dry thoroughly.

5. Fill with beans, although not too full. Sew up the opening left for inserting the beans neatly, but securely.

VARIATIONS

• Fill the bag with sand instead of beans and use as a display object or as a door stop.

• Fill the bag with cotton.

• Use a pinking shears for cutting out the main shapes.

Sunglass Case

A sunglass case is a gift for a Mom or another female. It offers a lot of possibilities for unique variations.

MATERIALS

—felt, various colors
—scissors (preferably both pinking shears and scissors that can cut felt easily)
—glue
—sequins (optional)
—toothpick
—needle and thread or sewing machine to make the case

PROCEDURE

1. The plain felt case should be made before the decorations are added. Be sure to make this case large enough to fit even the largest size sunglasses. Cut two pieces of felt in the shape of the case. Sew three sides together, ¼″ from the edge, with a needle and thread (or the teacher or volunteer can sew them all quickly on a sewing machine). (*Note:* Cutting the case shape out with a pinking shears is attractive.)

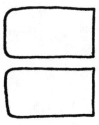

2. Sketch a design of how the front of the sunglass case will look on a piece of paper. Letters spelling the name of the sunglass owner can be artistically cut out of different colors of felt. Suggestions for other decorations are: butterflies, flowers, hearts, sun, and abstract shapes.

3. Cut out the various shapes of felt and glue to the plain sunglass case, using a toothpick to apply the glue.
4. Sequins can be applied in the same way on top of the colored felt shapes to add a sparkle. (*Note:* They could also be sewn on.)
5. Make sure everything is glued on securely.

VARIATIONS

• Stitch the sunglass case with colored yarn and a darning needle, using rather wide stitches.

Recipe Holder

This is a gift for a kitchen wall, or perhaps for the wall beside a telephone if it is relabeled "messages."

MATERIALS

—piece of wood, approximately 2" x 4" (oval shaped works well)
—wood clothespin (plastic could be substituted)
—glue
—enamel paint, spray can or brush
—felt pen, permanent ink, various colors of enamel paint, or felt scraps
—sandpaper

PROCEDURE

1. Sand the piece of wood. Then, center the clothespin on the front of the wood and glue down. Allow to dry throughly.

2. Paint the front and sides of the wood and the clothespin with enamel paint in any color desired—preferably a light color.

3. Add designs and/or words with colored permanent felt pens, other colors of enamel paint, or felt cut-outs.

4. To hang the little recipe holder—either nail the wood directly into the wall so it will remain stable, or nail a pop-top can ring to the back.

VARIATIONS

• Cut the letters RECIPES out of origami paper or construction paper and glue on the recipe holder.

Clay and Gravel Paper Weight

The addition of the colored aquarium gravel makes this little paper weight particularly unusual and interesting.

MATERIALS

—firing clay
—kiln in which to fire clay
—dark glaze and brush
—felt (to back paper weight)
—scissors
—glue
—fine sandpaper
—aquarium gravel in various colors (or white gravel and paints)
—non-stick surface to work on
—knife to cut the clay

PROCEDURE

1. Flatten out a small piece of clay (paper weight size) to be ½" to ¾" thick. Draw the outline of an object, such as a turtle, flower, or beetle, on it. Try to make the clay the same thickness all over.

2. Divide this object into several sections (where the aquarium gravel will later be glued).

3. Carve out the sections with the knife, carving ¼" into the clay. Leave a ridge all the way around the object and between the various sections.

4. After the clay has dried, sand it gently and bisque fire the clay in the kiln.

5. Paint the top and sides of the clay paper weight with a dark opaque glaze and allow to dry. Fire once again. (*Note:* Tempera paint could be substituted, along with a coat of shellac.)

6. Apply glue to the carved out sections of the paper weight and glue down aquarium gravel. Then, shake it to see that there are no loose grains. If white gravel is used, paint it with different colors of paint (watercolors will work). Allow this to dry.

7. Trace around the paper weight with a pencil on a small piece of felt. Cut this shape out and glue it to the back of the paper weight.

VARIATIONS

• Glue the clay and gravel object to a small piece of wood and use as a wall plaque.

• Use the Dough People recipe in the *Ornaments* section of this book instead of clay.

Papier Mache Napkin Rings

Papier mache napkin rings are a good beginning lesson in papier mache and make fun, interestingly shaped and colorful napkin rings. A set of four can be tied together with bright yarn to make a lovely gift.

MATERIALS

—paper towel or toilet paper rolls, or tagboard strips (5" x 1½") and masking tape (*Note:* Smaller children may have an easier time if the rings are larger in diameter than the commercial roll size. Rings can be made by securely fastening tagboard strips into a ring with masking tape.)
—strips of newsprint (5" x 1½")
—liquid starch or wheat paste and paper cups
—foil or waxed paper to work on and for rings to dry on
—tissue paper in various colors
—Polymer medium, P.V.A. and brush
—yarn, one-half yard per student

PROCEDURE

1. Jab a scissors into the roll and cut off a ring, 1½" wide. Repeat until each person has four rings in front of him.

2. Dip a newsprint strip into a cup of liquid starch, making sure the strip is completely wet. Wrap it around the ring, inside and out.

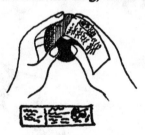

3. Continue applying the strips around the ring until none of the cardboard roll is visible. Use at least two layers of newsprint, being very careful to soak each strip in the starch. Smooth the edges. Allow to dry thoroughly.

4. Apply the tissue paper. Choose colors that look attractive together such as: red, yellow, orange, magenta; or blue, green, lavender. Tear the tissue paper into small, irregular pieces. Rub some starch on the ring with a finger and press on a piece of tissue paper. Continue doing this until every speck of the ring (inside and outside) is covered. Carefully wrap the tissue paper around the edges of the ring so that the edge is smooth and rounded. Go over the entire ring one final time with starch. Allow to dry on foil or waxed paper.

5. Brush Polymer medium or P.V.A. over the entire ring. Allow to dry until the napkin rings are no longer sticky to the touch.
6. Tie them together with a piece of yarn.

VARIATIONS

- Draw designs on the napkin rings with permanent felt pen after applying the tissue paper collage.
- Use one color of tissue paper instead of a variety of colors. Possibly use a different color for each of the napkin rings.
- Use newspaper instead of newsprint to give an interesting effect.

Clay Napkin Rings

Napkin rings are always a fun gift, particularly these rustic, unusual ones!

MATERIALS

—firing clay, preferably red
—kiln in which to fire clay
—glaze to paint on clay—one color will do (optional)
—rolling pins (optional)
—objects to add texture to the clay, such as buttons, hairpins, straw, pencils, nails, and screws
—a non-stick surface to work on, such as a piece of burlap
—plastic knife

PROCEDURE

1. Have each child work on a non-stick surface. Burlap will give the napkin rings a marvelous texture. Each child should be given about a 3" diameter ball of clay to make four napkin rings. (*Note:* A gift of two napkin rings would still be very nice.)
2. The clay can be rolled out with a rolling pin, but the palm of the hand could be used instead. Make sure that the clay is at least ¼" thick all over.
3. Use a knife to cut the clay into four strips, approximately 1½" wide, and 5" long.

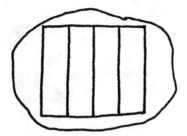

4. Scratch designs into these strips and add textures with the various objects.

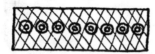

5. Roll the strips into cylinders and fasten together by pressing both sides together with fingers—smooth over this area, and add the textures over this joint.

6. Allow to dry in a cupboard.
7. Bisque fire in a kiln.
8. Paint on a glaze if desired. Or the napkin rings could be shined with P.V.A., Polymer medium, or wallpaper glaze.
9. Tie the rings together with a piece of rawhide or something similar before presenting as a gift.

VARIATIONS

• Rub shoe polish wax on the outside surface of the napkin rings (into the textures) and polish with a rag.

Felt Bookmark

There are limitless variations to this simple gift—tiny felt scraps, ribbons, and glue are all that is necessary to make these charming bookmarks.

MATERIALS

—various colors of felt scraps
—glue
—small sequins (optional)
—¼" grosgrain ribbon, 8" per bookmark
—scissors (sharp enough to cut felt easily)

PROCEDURE

1. Give the students various suggestions as to what they could make into a bookmark and let them give their suggestions as well, so that many ideas are floating around.
2. Sketch the idea on a small piece of paper.
3. Cut the shapes out of colored felt and make two copies of the largest, or main shape.

4. Glue the other pieces of felt on top of one of the main shapes. Add sequins for eyes or accents.

5. Glue the tip of the piece of grosgrain ribbon to the back of the first shape. Then place glue all over the back of this shape and stick the other main shape over this, so the tip of the grosgrain is hidden. Allow to dry thoroughly.

6. A smaller object could be made the same way and glued to the other tip of the grosgrain ribbon.

VARIATIONS

• Use leather thonging instead of the grosgrain ribbon.
• Stitch the two shapes together and stuff cotton inside for the felt part of the bookmark.

Plant in Handmade Pot

This simple pinch pot should delight anyone! Any small plant will look beautiful in this handmade pot (or a seed can be started and transferred into the pot before presenting it as a gift.)

MATERIALS

—firing clay
—glaze (optional)—one color will do
—kiln in which to fire clay
—objects to make textures in the clay, such as nails, screws, toothpicks, straws, buttons
—small plant, or seed, first planted in a paper cup

PROCEDURE

1. Give each student a 3″ in diameter piece of clay and have him work with it until all air bubbles have been removed.
2. Form the clay into a ball.
3. Use the thumbs to depress the beginning of what will be the center of the pot.

4. Establish the depth of the pot first by depressing the thumbs to approximately 3/8″ from the bottom.

5. To make the pot larger inside, gradually turn the pot with the thumbs inside while the clay is on a table. Carefully pinch the sides of the pot while rotating it.

6. Make sure the sides are not too thin but try to make the edges a uniform thickness.

7. Rub a finger around the top of the pot to make it smooth.

8. Make textures and designs on the outside of the pot with the objects.

9. Make a little hole in the bottom of the pot, as is seen in any flower pot. (*Note:* A coil pot, using "snakes" of clay, could also be used for this gift in place of the pinch pot method.)

10. When the pot has dried, bisque fire it (fire in a kiln for the first time).

11. Glaze the pot, if desired, and fire it in the kiln once again.

12. Transfer a plant, along with soil, into the little pinch pot before presenting it as a gift. A small sign, made with a toothpick and construction paper, can be placed in the soil next to the plant.

13. A ribbon may be tied around the pot to complete it.

VARIATIONS

• Fill the pot with an arrangement made of dried flowers and weeds.

• Fill the pot with small tissue paper or crepe paper flowers.

• Place a seed with soil in the pot and present it as a gift before the plant has sprouted, leaving an element of "surprise."

Letter Rack

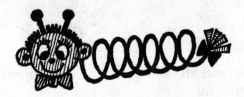

A letter rack can be a fun and comical gift, ideal for a Dad and extremely simple to make.

MATERIALS

—medium weight wire (the longer the wire, the longer the coil)
—cork wood block or styrofoam ball for a head
—felt scraps
—yarn
—glue
—scissors, sharp enough to cut felt
—something like a broom handle to form a coil with the wire

PROCEDURE

1. Take the piece of medium-weight wire and coil it around a broom handle, or something similar to form a coil. Leave about three inches of wire uncoiled at the end to form a tail, and a little bit at the beginning to stick into the head.

2. Make the head, using cork, a block of wood, or a styrofoam ball. Cut features out of felt and glue them on. Yarn can be used for hair. Use the imagination!

3. Attach the head to the coil. If styrofoam or cork is used, the beginning of the wire coil can be pushed into this. Or, if a piece of wood is used, a nail hole can be hammered into the wood in which the wire can be inserted. (*Note:* The first loop of the coil could be glued to the wood or the flat side of a cork instead.)

4. Add a tail—frayed yarn is one suggestion.

VARIATIONS

• Spray paint the entire letter rack with one color of enamel before decorating the head.
• Make the 'head' a felt flower with several layers of petals. Attach several leaves behind the petals.

Papier Mache Piggy Bank

This chubby piggy bank, a real labor of love, is a great challenge for children—an especially interesting art project.

MATERIALS

—one round balloon per student
—egg cartons (seven sections per pig)
—newsprint, torn into one-inch pieces
—newspaper to work on
—liquid starch and container for it
—colored tissue paper
—matt knife or sharp scissors
—permanent ink felt pens
—PVA, Polymer medium, or lacquer and brush

PROCEDURE

1. Blow up the balloon to the size desired and tie the end securely.
2. Tear newsprint into one-inch pieces and place in a heap on the newspaper.
3. Cover the balloon with the newsprint pieces dipped in liquid starch. Spread each piece of newsprint smoothly over the balloon, easing out bubbles of air, creases, and so on.

4. Repeat, covering the balloon with newsprint pieces about six times, making six layers. Do not cover the end of the balloon.

5. Cut individual sections from an egg carton for the feet, ears, and nose.
6. Position the four legs as shown and carefully cover them with many pieces of newsprint dipped in liquid starch so that they are part of the whole shape.

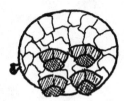

7. Leave to dry thoroughly.
8. Carefully deflate the balloon and pull it out of the hole.
9. Position the nose piece over the hole and cover it with pieces of newsprint dipped in liquid starch. Repeat for the ears. (*Note:* The ears could be cut out of felt and glued on the piggy bank at the end.)

10. Cover the pig with torn pieces of tissue paper dipped in liquid starch. Use a light shade of tissue paper if felt pens are to be used, or if a design cut out of colored tissue paper is to be added. Make sure that all edges are neatly pressed down. Allow to dry.

11. When dry, draw on eyes, nostrils and so on with felt pens. A decorative pattern may also be added.

12. If the pig is to be used for a bank, cut a slit out of the top with the matt knife or sharp scissors. A hole could be cut in the bottom of the bank and a cork inserted (if the bank is to be emptied).

13. Paint the entire pig with Polymer medium, PVA, or lacquer.

VARIATIONS

• Paint the piggy bank with spray paint and glue on felt features and decorations.

• Make other animals, such as an elephant, instead of the pig.

• A curled pipe cleaner could be used for the tail.

III–Gifts to Wear

Papier Mache Bracelet
Clay Beads
Bean and Seed Necklace
*Papier Mache Pin**
Little Clay People Pin
Tie-and-Dye Batik Scarf
Plaster of Paris Pin
Clay Pendant
*Metallic Pin**

* More Difficult—for third grade and above

Papier Mache Bracelet

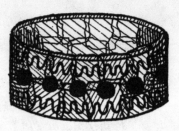

Here is an idea for "fun" jewelry that is simple enough for even the youngest child to make!

MATERIALS

—tagboard or cardboard strip, 1½" wide and long enough to go over the hand twice
—masking tape
—strips of newsprint, 1½" x 9" at least 1 dozen per bracelet
—wheat paste or liquid starch and container
—newspaper to work on
—colored tissue paper in various colors (approximately 9" x 12" piece per bracelet)
—felt pen, indelible or permanent type
—sequins and glue (optional)
—Polymer medium, P.V.A. and brush, or spray laquer
—foil, oil cloth, or waxed paper to set bracelets on to dry

PROCEDURE

1. Tape the tagboard strip securely with masking tape to make the bracelet shape. It will be stronger if the tagboard strip is doubled.

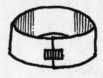

2. Soak the newsprint strips in liquid starch or wheat paste and apply to the tagboard bracelet. Wrap the strips around the bracelet, both ways, making sure to completely cover the inside and outside of the bracelet.

Repeat this many times until the bracelet is at least 1/8" thick.

3. Smooth all edges by rubbing liquid starch all over the bracelet.

4. Allow the bracelet to dry thoroughly.

5. Add the color: Tear colored tissue paper into small irregular shapes, dip them in liquid starch (or half white glue-half water mixture) and cover every inch of the bracelet. Use one color or several colors of tissue paper. Use a large brush or fingers to accomplish this. (*Note:* Good colors of tissue paper together are: hot pink and orange; blue and lavender; green and yellow.)

6. When the tissue paper has dried, decorate the bracelet with felt pen line designs, if desired. (*Note:* The felt pen must be indelible or permanent or it will "run" when the final, protective coating is applied.) Sequins may be glued on.

7. Paint the entire bracelet with Polymer medium, P.V.A., or spray with a spray laquer.

VARIATIONS

• Bracelets can be painted with acrylic paints and sequins of various sizes and colors can be glued on. Then the entire bracelet can be painted with Polymer medium.

Clay Beads

This type of necklace is an excellent example of primitive jewelry and children of any age can have fun creating clay beads.

MATERIALS

—one paper plate per child
—clay that hardens, at least a 2″ square piece per child
—nail
—gadgets such as buttons to add designs and textures to beads
—heavy duty thread, nylon thread, or fishing line
—needle
—wooden beads, macaroni, plastic straws (optional)
—opaque paints and small brush (tempera or acrylic paints)
—shellac in pan
—plastic knife
—aluminum foil, waxed paper, or oil cloth

PROCEDURE

1. Give all students a hunk of clay and have them make several dozen beads of varying sizes and shapes. Here are some methods for making clay beads:

   a) square beads: Make a flat square of clay and cut the clay with the knife into squares or rectangles. Put a hole through the middle of each bead with the nail.

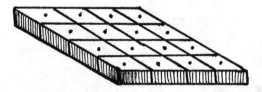

b) oblong beads: Roll out coils of clay and cut off units with the plastic knife. Put a nail hole through each bead.

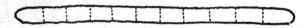

c) round beads: Make balls of clay by rolling and shaping them in the hands. Put a nail hole through each bead.

2. Add designs and textures to the beads with objects such as the head and point of the nail, buttons, or screws.

3. Give each child a paper plate with his name on it to store the beads while they dry completely.

4. Paint the beads. Use colors that go well together. If "red" clay was used to make the beads, leave some of the clay unpainted for an interesting, primitive effect. Tempera paint or acrylic paint can be used. (*Note:* Beads can first be painted with gesso and then painted with watercolors.)

5. String the beads. Separate the clay beads with wooden beads, macaroni, or small pieces of plastic straw. Make the necklace long enough to slip over the head.

6. After the necklace has been fastened together securely, the entire necklace can be dipped into a pan of shellac or lacquer. Allow the excess shellac to drip off of the beads into the pan. Place on foil to dry thoroughly before gift wrapping.

VARIATIONS

- Combine seeds and beans with the clay beads to make a necklace.
- Design a larger clay bead or pendant and string it in the middle of the necklace, with smaller beads on either side of it.
- Bisque fire all of the beads in a kiln. Then, rub shoe polish wax in different colors (i.e. red, black, brown) over the beads. After this has been done, wipe the beads until none of the shoe polish wax comes off on the fingers. The color of the wax will remain in the cracks that have been etched into the clay and leave a marvelous, rustic effect.

Bean and Seed Necklace

Making necklaces is an enjoyable project for both younger and older children, and quite a number of different-looking necklaces can be achieved.

MATERIALS

—various seeds and beans such as: garbonza and lima beans, watermelon and pumpkin seeds
—watermelon seeds
—pumpkin seeds
—macaroni (optional)
—heavy duty thread, nylon thread, or fishing line
—needle
—aluminum foil, waxed paper, or oil cloth
—paper plate to put seeds and beans in
—shellac and brush, or shellac in a container (optional)

PROCEDURE

1. Soak the seeds and beans in water to soften them and make the stringing of them easier. (Optional)
2. Thread a needle with a double thread long enough to fit over a head. Tie a small seed to the end of the thread to begin the string of seeds.
3. Alternate the various beans and/or seeds with the macaroni (if desired) to make an interesting pattern.

4. When the stringing of the seeds is completed, tie the string off carefully, making several knots so that the necklace is securely fastened together.

5. To shine the beads (Optional): Brush shellac over the entire necklace. Or, holding the necklace by a string attached to the necklace, dip it into a container of shellac. Remove the necklace and allow the excess shellac to drip back into the container. Place on foil to dry thoroughly before gift wrapping.

VARIATIONS

• For colored seeds, beans, and macaroni—place them in food coloring before stringing.

• Add other items such as wooden, glass, or clay beads to the seed necklace. Pieces of plastic straws can also make the necklace more interesting.

• Make a clay pendant as described on page 133 to hang in the center of the necklace.

Papier Mache Pin

What fun, cheerful jewelry this is! Children enjoy making these pins and it is a different type of lesson in papier mache.

MATERIALS

—tagboard or thin cardboard, 4" x 4" piece
—pattern of flower, leaf, heart, butterfly (optional)
—scissors
—small pieces of construction paper
—piece of newsprint (12" x 18")
—wheatpaste or liquid starch, and container for it
—foil, waxed paper, or oil cloth to dry pins on
—small pieces of tissue paper to color pins
—sequins in different colors and sizes (optional)
—Polymer medium to shine pins, shellac, or P.V.A. (and brush)
—glue
—pin backs (these sell for around 50¢ a dozen in a lapidary, hobby, or
　　crafts shop) and strong glue
—newspaper to work on

PROCEDURE

1. Cut desired shape for pin out of tagboard. One of the patterns may be traced or, even better, an original one can be drawn on the tagboard and cut out.

PATTERNS

2. Tear the newsprint into small pieces. Soak these pieces thoroughly in wheatpaste or liquid starch and stick to the tagboard shape. Cover both sides with many layers, and while tagboard is soft, bend the pin to desired shape. Petals of flowers, butterfly wings, and leaves may be bent upwards and small wads of tissue, paper towel, or newspaper may be placed under them to hold them in this position until they are dried completely.

3. Cover the entire shape with small, torn pieces of colored tissue paper. Use liquid starch and fingers to apply it. Allow this to dry.

4. Add accessories such as sequins and construction paper (for butterfly's body and center of flower). The butterfly's antennae can be made out of black wire or black cord glued to the back of the pin.

5. Glue the small pin back to the back of the pin with a strong glue.

6. Brush Polymer medium or PVA all over the pin to protect it as well as to give it a glossy appearance.

VARIATIONS

• Paint the pins with acrylic paints instead of applying tissue paper for color.

• Instead of putting the pin back on the objects, attach thread to them and hang three or more of them together as a mobile. Directions for balancing a mobile are shown on page 64.

Little Clay People Pin

Little clay creatures are fun to make and precious to own! They make a unique pin to wear on a dress, scarf, or purse. Note the other ways to use this idea described in the *Variations* section.

MATERIALS

—firing clay (red, preferably) 1½" ball per child
—paper towel to work on
—toothpick
—nail
—strainer or garlic press
—pin back (these sell for around 50¢ a dozen and are found in a lapidary, hobby, or crafts store) and strong glue
—glaze (white is attractive)
—black thin-lined felt pen (for making eyes)
—lipstick or pink chalk (for cheeks)
—strong glue to attach pin back
—kiln

PROCEDURE

1. Demonstrate how to go about making a little person: Form the clay into an oblong shape. Pinch it in for the neck and shape the head. Make three cuts in the clay with the nail, as shown, for the arms and legs. Then, pinch the arms and legs out and shape them. Remember that this must be tiny to wear as a pin.

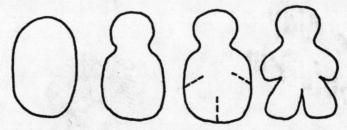

2. Poke two small holes for eyes, using the toothpick. Draw a curved line with the toothpick for the mouth.

3. Press a small ball of clay through a strainer (or garlic press) to make hair. Carefully remove this clay from the strainer with a toothpick. Attach this "hair" by gently pressing it to the front of the head of the little person with a toothpick. (*Note:* An animal can be created in a similar way.)

4. Let the clay dry thoroughly. (*Note:* Before the clay person begins to dry, make certain the back of it is flat, so it will be easy to attach the pin back.)

5. Bisque fire the objects. (This is the first firing in the kiln.)

6. Paint on the glaze. Don't cover all of the clay with the glaze; leave the hair and skin unglazed, and let the glaze serve as the "clothes," or for other accents.

7. Fire in the kiln once again.

8. Cheeks can be made rosy by rubbing a little lipstick or pink chalk into the clay. Eyes can be darkened with a thin-lined felt pen.

9. Attach the pin back to the clay person with a strong glue.

VARIATIONS

• Put a hole through the little clay creature, string rawhide, plastic lacing, or jute through it, and wear as a pendant.

• Flatten the back of the clay carefully and glue to a small, sanded and stained piece of wood. Attach a hanging loop to the top.

• Bisque fire the clay person or animal and then rub brown shoe polish all over the clay. Wipe most of this polish off with a piece of cloth, until no more comes off on the fingers.

Tie-and-Dye Batik Scarf

This scarf can be used in several ways: as a head scarf, as a headband, as a neck scarf, as a table decoration, or as a wall hanging. One warning—using dye can be messy, and is easiest when used with a small group at a time!

MATERIALS

—piece of old sheet, or muslin (handkerchief size) or an inexpensive handkerchief
—string
—scissors
—newspapers to work on
—dye (Rit Dye® works well) in red, blue, and yellow colors
—coffee cans to put dye in
—butcher paper
—iron
—tongs
—rubber gloves

PROCEDURE

1. The method for the tie-and-dye batik is a simple one—wherever a string is very tightly tied around the material, the dye will not go. And because the material is so wrinkled from being gathered so tightly, it is dyed in varying shades, making each scarf unique.

2. Tie two or more pieces of string around the gathered material. (*Note:* sheet or muslin squares would look more finished if they were hemmed. Perhaps a volunteer mother could do this for a class on her sewing machine.)

3. After the string ties have been added, it is time to dip the material into the three cans of dye. Rubber gloves will keep the hands from becoming dyed too! Tongs can be used to handle the material. One way to use the dye: Dip the entire tied material in yellow dye, or dip the material up to the second string tie in yellow dye. Then dip just the top (to the first string tie) in red or blue dye. Dip the bottom end (up to the second tie) in the final color.

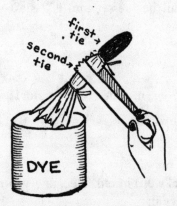

4. Allow to dry for several days. Then, clip the strings and open up the material. Iron it by placing a piece of butcher paper over the scarf. Use a hot iron. Although the pattern will be a circular one, the result is always an exciting surprise.

VARIATIONS

• Do not dip all of the material into the dye, but leave some of the fabric uncolored.

• Gather together two or three places on the scarf, tie these places with string, and dye in this manner. The result will be several circular patterns on the square scarf.

• Use a long, rectangular strip of fabric instead of the handkerchief shape and use as a wall hanging.

• Fold the material accordian-style and tie off several sections before dying.

Plaster of Paris Pin

Plaster of Paris pins are fun to wear on a dress, scarf, collar, or purse. They make delightful Mother's Day gifts.

MATERIALS

—plaster of Paris (1½ cups for approximately 30 pins)
—water (3/4 cup to mix with the plaster of Paris)
—coffee can (or other container) and mixing spoon
—measuring cup
—aluminum foil or waxed paper
—felt pens, watercolors, or tempera paints
—small brushes, if using paints
—pin backs (these sell for around 50¢ a dozen in a lapidary, hobby, or arts
    and crafts shop) and strong glue
—one large sheet of fine sandpaper
—clear nail polish

PROCEDURE

1. Pour ¾ cup water into a large container. Pour about 1½ cups plaster of Paris into the water, mixing constantly. Continue adding plaster of Paris until the mixture is like "soft ice cream." This will make about 30, 1½" in diameter pins, or ¾" balls.

2. Give each person a tablespoonful of the mixture on a piece of foil or waxed paper, and have them form it into a shape. (*Note:* Make sure all hands are clean before touching the plaster of Paris!) They must work quickly as the plaster of Paris can harden almost immediately. (*Note:* If an entire class is doing this project at one time, several "helpers" should be used to distribute the drops of plaster of Paris to each student so they may form it before it hardens.)

3. After the shapes are completely hard (in about thirty minutes), sand them, if necessary, to make them smooth. Just a tiny piece of sandpaper will do the job.

4. Have a sketch of what the pin will look like ready and lightly draw it on the plaster of Paris shape. Here are some ideas:

5. Color the design with felt pens or paint applied with a small brush. Take plenty of time!

6. Wait until the paint is dry before applying clear nail polish to the front and sides. (Clear nail polish works perfectly because of the small amount necessary to shine many such objects and because the brush is handy and will not need to be cleaned!)

7. When the front of the pin is dry, turn it over and glue on the pin back. Then, paint the entire back with clear nail polish.

(*Clean-Up Note:* Never pour plaster of Paris down the sink, as it will harden in the drainage pipe.)

VARIATIONS

• Make the shapes twice as large and use them as paper weights.
• Make the shape larger and glue to a sanded, stained piece of wood with a hanging ring on the top to use as a wall plaque.
• Put a piece of rawhide, plastic lacing, or jute through the pin back, and use as a pendant necklace.

Clay Pendant

Here is a simple lesson in working with clay for any age group, but the results are effective and lots of fun to wear. Shoe polish wax gives the clay a marvelous appearance!

MATERIALS

—small portion (approximately 1″ ball) of clay to be fired
—paper towel to work on
—nail
—buttons or other objects for making textures and designs in the clay
—kiln
—shoe polish wax in several colors (red, brown, black)
—small cloth
—rawhide, plastic lacing, thick yarn, or jute long enough for a necklace
    that slips over the head

PROCEDURE

1. Give each child a piece of clay, a nail, items to press into the clay, and a paper towel to work on. Have them make the pendant shape out of their clay. Make sure that the pendant is no thinner than 1/4 inch.

2. Make a hole at the top of the pendant with the nail.

3. Smooth the edges of the pendant to give it a "finished" look.

4. Make impressions and lines in the pendants with buttons, screws, and other items to add design and texture. The nail will be a good tool to use.

5. Have students put their initials on the back of the pendant so there is no confusion as to who the owner of each one is. Put the pendants away to dry. It may be necessary to place a flat object on top of them while they dry so they do not warp.

6. Bisque fire the pendants. (This is the first firing in the kiln.)

7. Rub shoe polish wax over the front of the pendant, making sure it gets down into the crevices and into all the lines etched into the pendant. After this has been done, wipe the pendant thoroughly until none of the shoe polish wax comes off on the fingers. The result will be a rustic, rich-looking pendant with textures and patterns highlighted with a dark color.

8. Attach the rawhide, plastic lacing, yarn, or jute to the pendant. Knot it at the nail hole so the pendant hangs properly.

VARIATIONS

• Bisque fire the pendants. Then paint them with "Bisq-wax"® (found in ceramic stores) and a small brush. Bright colors are available.

• Leave the pendants their natural clay color, but apply a coat of clear or colored glaze to the front of the pendant and fire in the kiln. This will make them very shiny.

• Paint the fired pendants with Polymer medium or shellac.

Metallic Pin

It looks like sterling silver with a raised relief pattern; and with black accents, it's hard to believe it is made out of cardboard and aluminum foil!

MATERIALS

—cardboard (approximately 5" x 7")
—scissors
—glue
—aluminum foil (approximately 5" x 5")
—matt black spray paint, India ink, or black powder paint (Mixed with liquid detergent and brush)
—a very small piece of fine steel wool
—pin back (these sell for around 50¢ a dozen and are found in a lapidary, hobby, or crafts store) and strong glue
—small piece of construction paper or felt for back of pin

PROCEDURE

1. Decide on a shape for the pin—oval, round, square, diamond, free-form, or the shape of some object such as a flower, butterfly, or fish.

2. Cut this shape out of the cardboard twice and glue together for added thickness.

3. Cut out smaller shapes to be glued to the pin shape to make a relief. Place them on top of the shape, one on top of the other to build the design up. The more cardboard shapes, the thicker and more three-dimensional the pin will be. (*Note:* Building the pin up to 1/8″ at its highest point would be ideal.)

4. Glue each cardboard shape down and allow to dry.

5. Apply glue to the front side of the pin and place it face down in the middle of the foil square. Carefully smooth the foil over the raised sections and into the hollows, working from the center outwards. Smooth over the edges and glue to the back of the pin.

6. With a ballpoint pen or pencil, etch lines on the front of the pin to add more texture.

7. Place all of the pins on newspaper (preferably outside of the classroom) and lightly spray them with the black matt spray, or paint them with either India ink or black powder paint mixed with liquid detergent.

8. When they are dry, gently rub the paint off of the raised sections of the pin with fine steel wool. Work carefully and slowly or the foil may tear.

9. Cut a piece of felt or construction paper a fraction smaller than the shape of the pin and glue to the back of the pin. With strong glue, attach the small pin back to the middle of this.

VARIATIONS

• To simplify the pins, do not build up the cardboard, but glue the foil to the cardboard shape and add the design and texture by etching it into the foil with a ballpoint pen or pencil. Work carefully so the foil will not tear. Paint black ink over the foil and rub part of it off with steel wool.

• Draw a free design on the cardboard pin shape with white glue or dribble it on in various places. Allow this glue to dry. The glue will be raised enough to give the pin the relief pattern. Cover with foil and complete the project as described above.

IV–Gifts to Display

Piled and Painted Stones
Acorn Mouse
Collage Vase
Crepe Paper Flower *
Gold Macaroni Tree
Pellon Doll
Toothpick Sculpture
Wood Sculpture
Pine Cone Creature
Felt Nosegay

*More difficult—for third grade and above.

Piled and Painted Stones

Rounded, smooth stones put together in an interesting way provide a fun to make as well as fun to give present.

MATERIALS

—pebbles and stones of various sizes and shapes
—strong glue
—white acrylic paint (one tube per class should do) and small brush
—several sets of colored felt pens
—crayons
—Polymer medium, P.V.A., or shellac and brush (optional)
—paper towel to work on
—bits of fur, yarn, or other items for accents

PROCEDURE

1. Wash the stones and dry completely before beginning the project.
2. Arrange a few stones together to create a creature or some abstract form. (A single stone could be used.) When the arrangement of the stones satisfies the student, place strong glue on two stones and press together. Hold with hands until the glue has begun to adhere. Allow the glue to dry

completely before attempting to paint the form. Make certain the stone form will stand up by itself.

3. Decorate the stones with a combination of white acrylic paint (and/or other colors, although white is very effective on the stone), felt pens, and crayon (which gives an interesting, textured appearance when rubbed over the stones). Do not try to make something look too realistic, but create a fantasy character.

4. Brush on a final coat of Polymer medium to shine and protect the stones.
5. Add bits of fur, yarn or other items for accents if desired.

VARIATIONS

- Glue the stone creature to a wooden, sanded and stained base.
- Glue a few pebble creatures (such as owls) to a piece of driftwood.
- Do not paint the stones at all, but glue several of them on top of one another for an unusual piece of natural sculpture.

Acorn Mouse

If acorns are available, this unusual little project makes a sweet gift for anyone. Each mouse takes on his own distinctive personality!

MATERIALS

—small piece of wood, approximately 1½" x 3" (1/4" thick)
—sandpaper, small piece (2" square) per person
—1" piece of brown construction paper
—1½" piece of brown yarn or thin strip of leather (for tail)
—black thin-lined felt pen
—glue
—toothpick for applying glue
—scissors
—paper towel to work on
—acorn, one per student
—three 2-inch pieces of thread (preferably "heavy duty thread")

PROCEDURE

1. Sand the piece of wood and write name or initials on bottom side.
2. Glue the shiny acorn, minus "cap," to the wood.
3. Cut out two small ears as shown. Glue them near the pointed end of the acorn, using a drop of glue on a toothpick. Bend up the ears.

4. Glue the yarn or leather tail underneath the opposite end of the acorn.

5. Add eyes with a black, thin-lined felt pen.

6. Place a tiny dot of glue on mouse's nose and add three 2-inch pieces of thread for whiskers.

7. Other accessories, such as a bow, may be added to complete the little acorn mouse.

VARIATIONS

- Glue two acorn mice to the wooden stand.
- Make the ears out of brown leather as well as the tail.
- Paint a small piece of cork yellow and glue it in front of the mouse's face to resemble a piece of swiss cheese.
- Small glass beads may be used for the mouse's eyes.
- Make other animals in the same way (e.g., rabbit).

Collage Vase

A useful vase is a result of this quick project in tissue paper collage.

MATERIALS

—jar, bottle, or can
—newsprint
—tissue paper in various colors
—liquid starch and container or half white glue-half water mixture
—brush
—newspaper to work on
—Polymer medium, P.V.A., or shellac and brush

PROCEDURE

1. Select any shaped bottle, jar or can for the vase. Make certain it is washed and dried thoroughly before beginning.

2. Tear some newsprint into irregular pieces. Apply some liquid starch or half white glue-half water mixture to the bottle with a brush and stick a piece of newsprint to the bottle. (*Note:* Wheat paste could be used for this step.) Fingers could be used instead of a brush. Continue in this manner until the entire outside of the bottle has been covered with newsprint. Work around the top of the bottle with newsprint, sticking the pieces to the inside of the neck as well.

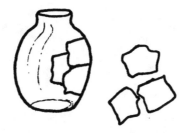

3. Tear pieces of tissue paper into irregular pieces. Apply these over the newsprint, covering it completely. Use several colors of tissue paper. (*Note:* Good color combinations: hot pink, magenta, lavender; orange, gold, yellow; olive green, chartreuse, yellow.) Make sure the tissue paper covers the neck inside. Allow to dry.

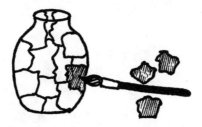

4. Brush Polymer medium, P.V.A. or shellac over the vase to give it a protective and glossy coat.

5. Put some paper flowers, straw flowers, or garden flowers in the vase before presenting it as a gift.

VARIATIONS

• Use printed newspaper instead of plain newsprint for the first layer on the vase. The print will show through the tissue paper for a different effect.
• Use one color of torn tissue paper on the vase. Then cut or tear out a design using several other shades of tissue paper, and apply this design on top of the single color of tissue paper.
• Omit the first layer of newsprint on the vase and use only tissue paper for a transparent look.
• Apply the newsprint pieces to the bottle. Then glue cord or thick string on top of this in a design or pattern. Allow this to dry. Apply tissue paper pieces over the newsprint and cord, carefully pressing the tissue paper down where the cord makes a bump.

Crepe Paper Flowers

Crepe paper flowers are gay, simple, and fun to make. A single flower makes a very nice gift.

MATERIALS

—9″ x 6″ pieces of crepe paper, three pieces per flower
—thin wire, easily bendable, one foot per flower
—reed (used in weaving reed baskets) or other thin stick, about one foot long per flower
—green stem tape, about one yard per.flower. (This is sticky tape and can be purchased in a hobby shop or possibly obtained at a florist shop.)
—3″ x 4″ pieces of green crepe paper, two per flower

PROCEDURE

1. Place the three colored pieces of 9″ x 6″ crepe paper on top of each other and fold them accordian-style. Make sure they remain on top of one another. Three different colors of tissue paper look beautiful. Watch which way the crepe paper "stretches."

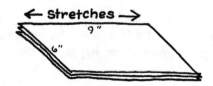

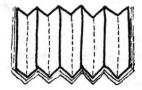

2. After the folding is done, find the middle of the folded paper and wrap the wire around this spot. Leave the ends of the wire unwrapped. (*Note:* Both ends of this folded paper can be rounded using a scissors.)

3. Put the reed (stem) next to this middle spot and wrap the remainder of the wire around the reed until the paper is attached securely to the reed.

4. Place the green tape beside the top of the reed where the tissue paper has been attached with wire. Wind the green tape tightly around the wire several times. Then continue down the reed (stem), with the tape, stretching the green tape as it is wound around the reed.

5. Stop winding half way down the stem in order to add leaves. First, cut out two leaf shapes (as shown), using the green crepe paper. Gather the

straight end of the leaf by hand. Place this gathered end of the leaf beside the reed stem. Do the same with the second leaf and place it near the first leaf. Continue wrapping the stem tape around the ends of the leaves several times to securely fasten them to the stem.

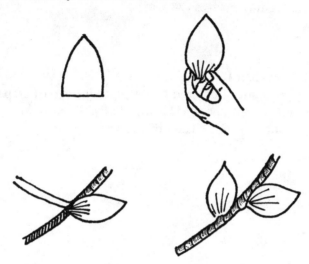

6. Wrap the green stem tape around the reed until the bottom of the stem is reached. Fasten off at the bottom carefully so the tape will not begin to unwind itself. (*Note:* If green stem tape is not available, thin strips of green crepe paper (that stretch) can be substituted, but will have to be glued or taped at the bottom of the stem.)

7. To form the flower: Spread out the accordian-folded crepe paper, as shown.

8. Then, separate each of the three layers of crepe paper so each layer stands slightly apart. Gently stretch the top edge of the crepe paper to curl it and give the look of petals. Carefully push outwards from the inside of the crepe paper flower to further stretch and shape it.

9. Stretch and form the leaves the same way.

VARIATIONS

• Make the flowers half this size.

• Make the flowers out of colored tissue paper instead of crepe paper. The effect will be a different one, but beautiful as well, particularly as all three layers are different colors or shades of the same color.

Gold Macaroni Tree

An ornate macaroni tree makes an attractive centerpiece for a table.

MATERIALS

—tagboard or cardboard (enough for half of a 10" diameter circle for cone
    and a 4" circle for base)
—masking tape
—scissors
—empty spool of thread, one per tree
—macaroni in different shapes (such as shell, bow, wheel, and star)
—gold spray paint
—gold glitter
—newspaper to work on
—container to hold macaroni
—white glue

PROCEDURE

1. Make the tree shape out of the tagboard. Bend the half-circle around, overlapping the two ends to make a 4-inch base on the cone. Tape the cone in several places with masking tape. Cut out a 4-inch circle and tape it to the bottom of the cone. Tape this in about four places so the cone is fastened together securely.

2. Glue the spool to the bottom of the cone (on the 4-inch base) in the exact center. This serves as the "tree trunk." Make sure that the tree will stand up straight.

3. Glue on the macaroni, making sure to cover every inch of the tagboard. Cover the bottom edge of the cone with macaroni.

4. Allow the glue to dry thoroughly. Gently shake the tree to see if any pieces of macaroni fall off. If so, glue them on again. Some small pieces of macaroni can be glued on top of larger pieces.

5. Cover the trees from top to bottom with gold spray paint. (*Note:* Trees of an entire class can be sprayed quickly at one time, preferably outside on newspaper.)

6. While the paint is wet, sprinkle glitter over the gold paint. Allow to dry completely. Then, shake the tree gently to get loose glitter off.

VARIATIONS

• Spray paint the tree another color, using spray enamel. Sprinkle on glitter of the same color or a color that complements the tree.

• Cover a small orange juice can with macaroni in the same manner to use as a pencil holder.

Pellon Doll

A classroom filled with pellon dolls is a sight to see! No two turn out alike in size, shape, or look. Here is a precious example of each "artist's" style to be kept forever.

MATERIALS

—pellon fabric available in any fabric store. It is a white, semi-stiff material which comes in various qualities. The least expensive works well. (Three yards of pellon should be more than enough for 30 dolls, approximately 10″ tall.)
—needle and white thread
—crayons, felt pens, or colored chalk
—stuffing for doll: cotton, polyester filling, nylon stockings, or tissues
—scissors
—yarn for hair (optional)
—iron and butcher paper if crayon is used
—scratch paper and pencil

PROCEDURE

1. Draw a person (perhaps a portrait of someone special) on a piece of scratch paper, the same size that the doll will be. Cut the shape out.
2. Transfer this idea to a piece of pellon, using a pencil.

3.   Color in the outline, using crayons, felt pens, or colored chalk. Work on a piece of newspaper. Color all parts of the doll's front view, paying attention to every detail. Rosy cheeks add to the coloring of the face.

4.   If crayon was used, place the doll between two pieces of butcher payer and iron (with a hot iron) the two sides of the doll.

5.   Put this colored piece of pellon on top of another piece of pellon and pin the two pieces together.

6.   With a needle and thread, sew around the outline of the front view of the doll, leaving a large enough opening at the top of the head for stuffing the doll. Use a running stitch.

7.   Cut around the outline of the doll, ¼" from the stitching. (*Note:* Pellon is a good material to use for this project as it does not ravel, is easy to draw on, and easy to sew on.)

8.   Color the back side of the doll just as the front was done.

9.   Stuff the doll, using the opening at the top of the head. A pencil can help to push the stuffing material to the various parts of the doll. The doll does not need to be too "round," but about 1/2" thick all over.

10. Pieces of yarn, for fun hair, may be placed in the opening at the top of the head before it is sewed up. Sew up the doll and fasten off the thread securely.

VARIATIONS

- Accessories may be added to the doll, such as ribbon, buttons, flowers, sequins.
- The doll may be "dressed" in clothes made out of printed fabrics and/or felt (sewed with a needle and thread).
- Make the doll out of felt instead of pellon (a light color may be colored on with chalk or felt pen.)

Toothpick Sculpture

Here is a great little art project for a rainy day and a cute idea for a gift. It is amazing how many different-looking structures will evolve out of this simple technique.

MATERIALS

—a box of toothpicks per student (let each provide his own)
—white glue
—6" x 6" piece of aluminum foil or waxed paper to work on
—small piece of wood for base of sculpture
—sandpaper to smooth base
—stain for wood (optional)
—pieces of colored tissue

PROCEDURE

1. Put a small amount of glue on a toothpick and place on another toothpick. (*Note:* One toothpick can be used as the glue applicator.) Work on the piece of aluminum foil or waxed paper. Toothpicks may be glued onto each other, across each other, or any way possible. Sometimes it is necessary to hold the two toothpicks together for a few minutes until the glue has begun to dry, or brace them with other, unglued toothpicks. After the initial toothpicks have been glued together, it becomes much easier to add further toothpicks. Continue gluing toothpicks to other

toothpicks, creating a three-dimensional structure. It may or may not resemble something. Let the imagination run wild!

2. Sand the wooden base and stain it, if desired. Glue the completed structure to this base.

VARIATIONS

- Various colored toothpicks could be used.
- Paint the entire sculpture, including the wooden base. A spray paint such as a black matt finish looks interesting.
- After the toothpick structure is completed and glued to the base, a dash of color may be added with tissue paper. Sections of the structure may be "filled in" with tissue paper. Cut the tissue paper to fit the shape made by the toothpicks. Trim the piece until it fits perfectly before gluing it. Carefully place the glue (using a toothpick applicator) on one side of the toothpicks and gently place the trimmed tissue paper over this. Tissue paper covering several small areas is most effective.
- Use a small block of styrofoam as the base. Poke the first toothpicks into it and glue the rest of the structure to these.

Wood Sculpture

This is one of the greatest first adventures in three-dimensional "building" art and appropriate for any age.

MATERIALS

—scraps of wood in various sizes and shapes. (*Note:* Carpenter shops, lumber stores, and new home sights are suggestions as to where scraps of wood may be obtained for this project.)
—sandpaper (optional)
—white glue
—newspaper
—shellac (optional)
—tempera paint and brush (optional)

PROCEDURE

1. Select pieces of wood in different sizes and experiment with them as building blocks. As with building blocks, arms can extend out from the center, as long as the center of balance is through the base. The design can be regular and repetitive, very organized or random.
2. The pieces of wood chosen to be used in the sculpture can be sanded, although it is not at all necessary.
3. To join the wood: Apply glue lightly to the two surfaces to be joined.

Allow this glue to dry for a few minutes. Add a little more glue, spread thin, and hold the two pieces of wood together for a few minutes, until the glue is set. By this simple procedure, pieces of wood can be glued on to each other, across other pieces, overlapping, and so on.

4. Continue adding to the design until the result is a pleasing sculpture. It may be necessary to glue the structure on a base (or it may be easier to begin gluing the wood scraps to a base.)

5. To complete the wood sculpture: This may be accomplished in various ways:

1) Rub an oil (such as linseed oil) over the entire sculpture with a small rag.
2) Shellac the wood with a brush.
3) Paint the wood with various colors of tempera paint.
4) Leave the wood natural.

Pine Cone Creature

If pine cones can be found, try making pine cone creatures for a centerpiece decoration or hanging from a doorway or ceiling.

MATERIALS

—pine cones, in perfect condition—one per student
—pieces of colored felt
—construction paper pieces
—pieces of yarn
—cotton
—scissors
—glue
—buttons, sequins, or other items
—newspaper to work on
—toothpick for applying glue
—cardboard or wood

PROCEDURE

1. Glue the pine cone to a base. This may be cardboard "feet" glued to the base of the pine cone, or the pine cone glued to a block of wood. (*Note:* The wider end of the pine cone should be glued to the base.) Allow to dry thoroughly.

2. Decide what features will be added to the pine cone to give it a special "identity." Cut these out of pieces of colored felt or construction paper. These features can be glued directly to the pine cone. Arms can be stuck into the pine cone. Add cotton or yarn for the hair. Sequins may be glued to circles of felt or construction paper to make eyes sparkle. Hats do a lot to add "personality" to the pine cone creature. (*Note:* Arms sticking out from the pine cone are effective, particularly when they are holding something. Signs can be made out of a piece of construction paper glued to a toothpick.)

VARIATIONS

- Owls are fun and easy to make out of pine cones. Use three different-sized felt circles for the eyes and glue a felt beak between them. Add construction paper or felt wings, which stand away from the pine cone. Claws can be added to the base.
- Spray paint the pine cone with a colored spray lacquer before decorating.
- Use only items from nature to glue on the pine cone, such as pebbles, shells, dried flowers, nuts, seeds, leaves, and twigs.

Felt Nosegay

These extremely simple little flowers make a sweet and colorful nosegay, most appropriate for any occasion!

MATERIALS

—pipe cleaners, preferably green (one per flower)
—pieces of colored felt
—scissors to cut the felt (pinking shears make nice edges on the flowers)
—a sharp object to jab a hole through the felt
—paper doilie (one per nosegay)
—ribbon to complete the nosegay (about 15″ per nosegay)

PROCEDURE

1. Cut out three circles of felt. The patterns may be used. Put good color combinations together.

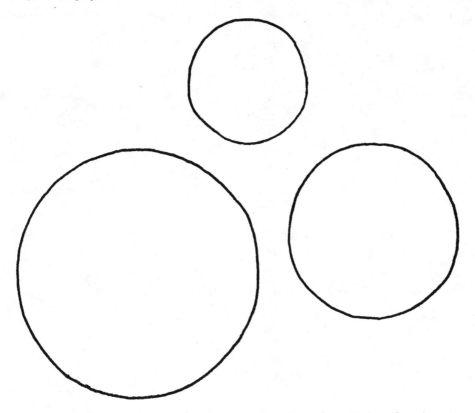

2. Jab a hole through the centers of the three felt circles (for the pipe cleaner).

3. Put the three circles on the pipe cleaner. Bend the tip of the pipe cleaner over to hold the felt circles on. The pipe cleaner can be curled to serve as the "stamen" of the flower.

4. Make other flowers (different-colored) using this method.

5. Poke the ends of the pipe cleaner stems through the center of a paper doilie. Tie a ribbon tightly around the doilie and pipe cleaners so the nosegay will stay together.

VARIATIONS

- Use felt flower shapes instead of circles to make the flowers.
- Use fabric (small prints) instead of the felt to make the flowers.
- Use paper instead of felt for the flowers.

V–Paper Gifts

Poetry Book
Oriental Scrapbook *
Felt Pen Notecards
Clipboard
Recipe Book
Initial Notecards *
Calendar
Printed Notecards

* More Difficult—for third grade and above

Poetry Book

Combining language arts with art makes a very meaningful gift, certain to be treasured by the receiver.

MATERIALS

—one or more poems by each member of the class. Students (or teacher) transfer these poems to a ditto master and enough copies are run off for each student's poetry book.
—two pieces of cardboard, each 6" x 9"
—tissue paper in various colors
—half white glue-half water mixture and container
—newspaper to work on
—brush
—construction paper
—scissors
—glue
—paper punch
—yarn

PROCEDURE

1. Make the cover by covering two pieces of cardboard with torn pieces of tissue paper in various colors. Attach the tissue paper to the cardboard with the glue mixture. Cut off the tissue paper hanging over the edges.

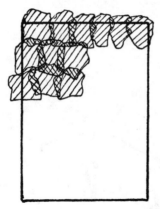

2. Cut out or tear the word *POEMS* or another fitting title from a piece of construction paper and glue to the front cover.

3. The book may have a title page that can also be put on a ditto master. This page can also be decorated with the torn tissue paper collage.

4. Punch two holes in each of the cardboard covers and in all pages of poems. Tie the book together with two pieces of yarn.

VARIATIONS

• Make a leaf rub and glue it to the cardboard covers in place of the tissue paper collage. To make the rub: Place fresh leaves under white drawing paper and (using the side of crayon) rub over the leaves until the imprint of the leaves shows up on the paper. Repeat this technique with several colors of crayon. Hold the paper tightly with one hand while rubbing with crayons, so the leaves underneath do not move.

• Watercolor paint the cover by dabbing a sponge into paint and onto the paper, creating a delicate, textured cover. Use a variety of colors. A 1" square sponge works well. The paint should not be too wet.

Oriental Scrapbook

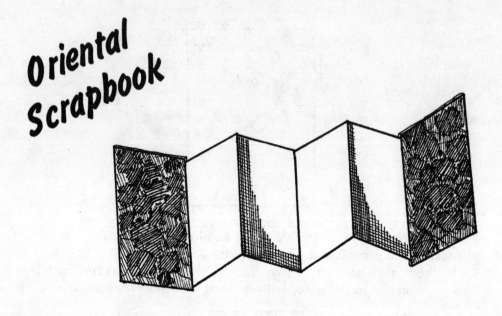

Here is an unusual gift, fashioned after the Oriental scrapbook with its accordian style of folding. It could be used as a photo album, poetry book, or practically anything.

MATERIALS

—two pieces of cardboard—4½" x 5½" is a good size
—glue
—strip of paper, 24" x 5" (if the cover is 4½" x 5½") It can be longer if more pages are desired. Butcher, tagboard, or construction paper will do.
—white paper to paint on
—water and container
—brush
—scissors
—newspaper to work on
—ruler

PROCEDURE

1. Make the painting for the cover of the book first. This could be accomplished in a variety of ways. Here are several techniques that will make attractive covers:

a) Wet-into-wet painting on crinkled paper: Place the paper in a pan of water or under the faucet and soak completely. Then, wad up the paper so it is full of wrinkles. Open it up, flatten it out, and place it on a piece of newspaper. While the paper is still very wet, apply watercolors in "blobs" with a rather large brush. This paint will run and form interesting, cloud-like shapes. The colors will appear deeper in the cracks made by wadding up the paper. After ironing the painting, it will make an absolutely fascinating cover for the little book.

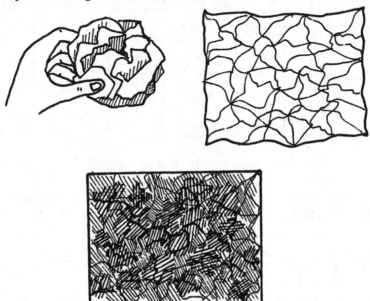

b) Blow painting: Add water to the watercolor paints to make them quite wet, but still rich in color. Use the paint brush to place dots of this paint on the paper. Put the tip of the straw next to the dot of paint, and blow through it. Follow the paint as it spreads out, blowing at the same time. Tip the paper to aid the paint in spreading over the paper. Use a variety of colors that go well together. Let the painting dry completely and iron the back of it with a hot iron.

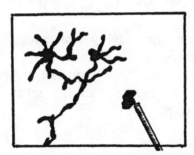

2. Cover the cardboard: Place one piece of the cardboard on top of the back side of the painted paper. Trace around it with a pencil and leave a 1-inch margin all the way around the cardboard. Fold the four corners as shown. Then, fold the sides of the painting on the pencil line and glue all of these edges to the cardboard. Press under several heavy books.

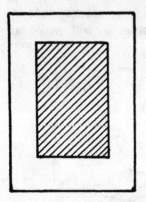 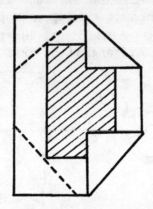 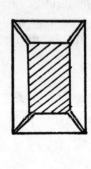

3. Add the pages: Mark off the long strip of paper at 4-inch intervals with the ruler. Fold them very carefully in accordian-style. Glue the two ends of this folded paper to the backs of the two covers, centering them carefully. Press under several heavy books until the glue is completely dry.

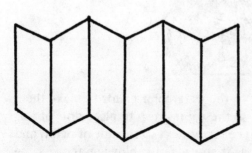 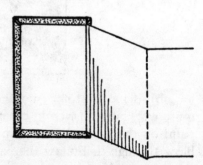

VARIATIONS

• Tissue paper collage the cardboard, as described in the *Poetry Book* gift idea on page 166.
• Make a design using crayon or felt pen on construction paper to glue to the cardboard, and use these as the covers.
• Cover the cardboard covers with Oriental newspaper and glue on a design cut out of tissue paper. Paint the entire cover with Polymer medium, P.V.A., or lacquer.

Felt Pen Notecards

What a treat to receive a packaged selection of hand-drawn notecards by a favorite artist to use for that "special" occasion, or to frame!

MATERIALS

—several sets of multi-colored felt pens
—white drawing or construction paper, 6" x 7" per card (folded to be 6" x 3½" cards). (*Note:* One piece of 12" x 18" construction paper will make four notecards.)
—envelopes (Most dime stores, grocery stores, and drug stores carry a very inexpensive 3 5/8" x 6 1/2" business envelope. A box of 100 envelopes is available.)
—cellophane or clear food wrap
—Scotch Tape®
—a small square of paper to enclose in the package.

PROCEDURE

1. Motivate "artists" by asking for suggestions of what could be drawn on the notecards. Encourage each person to draw what they like best to draw, but give examples such as: people, animals, fish, abstract designs, landscapes, stylized suns, butterflies, bugs, flowers, and so on.
2. It might be easiest to begin with a border, approximately ½" from the

edge of the paper, drawn with a felt pen. For very young students, the teacher may choose to do this.

3. Draw pictures on the front of the notecards. It might be fun to stick with one theme, such as animals. Remind everyone to use lots of color and have fun, being as imaginative as they can.

4. Make a little sign, using a thin-lined felt pen, ink pen, typewriter, or colored pencil, stating what is in the package.

5. How to package the notecards: Select a favorite notecard to place on top, with the other three cards under it. The four envelopes will be under the cards. Place the little card telling what is in the package in a visible spot. Cover with cellophane or clear food wrap and tape the ends neatly on the back.

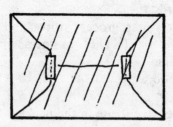

VARIATIONS

- The drawings may be made on white paper, cut out, and glued onto pastel construction paper.
- Paints or crayons may be used instead of felt pens.

Clipboard

These cheerful clipboards can be made any size and be used in the kitchen for shopping lists, by the phone, or hung by the door for messages.

MATERIALS

—chip board or cardboard, rectangular-shaped, any size desired
—tissue paper in various colors
—half water-half glue mixture and container for it
—brush
—Polymer medium, P.V.A. or spray lacquer (optional)
—clip (about 3¢ each in a school supply catalog)
—several sheets of paper to clip on clipboard
—small bits of colored felt and glue (optional)
—newspaper to work on
—scissors
—newsprint (to tear up and glue to cardboard)

PROCEDURE

1. Glue two pieces of cardboard together for added thickness. Press under several heavy books and allow to dry.

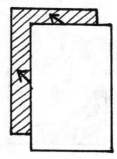

2. Tear pieces of newsprint into irregular shapes. Glue them to the cardboard using the half water-half glue mixture and a brush. Cover the cardboard completely, front and back. Cover the sides as well.

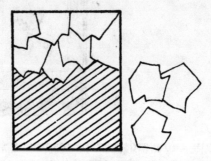

3. While the newsprint is still wet from the glue solution, cover the entire piece with torn shapes of tissue paper in several colors. Brush the half glue-half water mixture over them. Allow the covered cardboard to dry. (*Note:* Teacher can put the clip on the cardboard and hang on a line to dry.)

4. Polymer medium or PVA can be brushed on the clipboard while it hangs on the line, or spray lacquer can be sprayed all over the clipboard. Allow to dry completely. (*Note:* It is not necessary to add this step, as the half water-half glue mixture will give the clipboard a semi-glossy finish.)

5. Cut small designs out of pieces of colored felt, and glue onto the border of the clipboard. (optional)

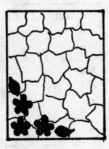

6. Clip several pieces of paper to the board before presenting it as a gift.

VARIATIONS

• Cover the cardboard with torn pieces of newspaper first and apply pieces of tissue paper over this. The newspaper print will show through the tissue paper for an interesting effect.

Recipe Book

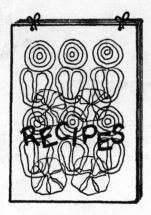

Here is a project in which Mother takes part. She donates her favorite recipe (as does every other child's mother) and later receives a handmade recipe book with a special recipe from the mother of every class member. The cover is an exciting lesson in vegetable printing.

MATERIALS

—two pieces of 9″ x 6″ cardboard
—two pieces of 9″ x 12″ construction paper
—two pieces of 8½″ x 5½″ colored construction paper
—vegetables and fruits, such as carrots, green peppers, celery stalks, onions, and citrus fruits
—thick tempera paint and brush. Use several colors of paint.
—paper for trial prints
—several thicknesses of newspaper to work on to create a padded surface when printing
—small aluminum pans for the paint
—glue
—thick yarn
—paper punch
—copies of each recipe run off on the duplicating machine

PROCEDURE

1. Cut all the fruits and vegetables in half and leave upside down to dry for an hour.

2. Brush the thick paint on the sliced vegetable or fruit and press it down on the construction paper (9″ x 12″ size). White, yellow or pastel colors are very attractive as the background. Try to make an interesting design with the vegetable and fruit impressions. Work on a pad of newspapers and practice printing on other paper before printing the final cover.

3. To make the cover: Place one piece of the cardboard on top of the painted paper. Trace around it with a pencil, leaving a margin all the way around it. Fold the four edges as shown. Then fold the sides of the painting on the pencil lines, and glue all of the edges to the cardboard. Press under several heavy books. Repeat with the other piece of cardboard and painting.

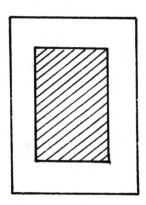
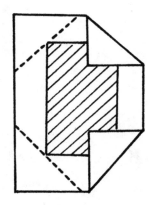
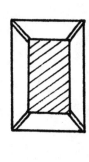

4. Glue a piece of colored construction paper (8½" x 5½" size) to the back of each covered cardboard to give the cover a "finished" look.

5. Now, for what's inside the book! Have each child collect his mother's favorite recipe. Retype each of the recipes on a ditto master, and run off enough copies for each child's recipe book. Add something such as: "from Tom Jackson's Mom" at the bottom of each recipe. The recipe book may be divided into sections (*Salads* and *Desserts*). Pages to separate each section may be added with further vegetable or fruit prints. Students may want to write the section titles with thick-lined felt pens.

6. Punch two holes at the top of both cardboard covers and each page of recipes. Tie together with two pieces of yarn. Tie them rather loosely so that the pages of the book will turn easily.

VARIATIONS

• Cover two pieces of cardboard with colorful fabric and write the title with alphabet macaroni, to be used as the cover for the recipe book.

• Make a collage of all types of food cut out of magazines to be glued on the cardboard for the cover of the recipe book.

Initial Notecards

There are numerous ways to make notecards, and it is hoped that this method will lead to the discovery of other ideas. By incorporating the initial of the person who is to receive the gift, the cards become highly personalized.

MATERIALS

—white drawing paper notecards (6" x 7" paper per card, folded to become 6" x 3½" cards). One piece of 12" x 18" construction paper will make four notecards.
—felt pens (several sets per class)
—or colored chalk and spray fixative (*Note:* An inexpensive hair spray is much cheaper and works equally as well to set the chalk.)
—or crayons
—envelopes (Most dime stores, grocery stores, or drug stores carry a very inexpensive 3 5/8" x 6 1/2" business envelope. A box of 100 envelopes is available.)
—directions for packaging the cards are given in the *Felt Pen Notecards* idea on page 171.

PROCEDURE

1. Select an appropriate initial to use for the basis of the design. Sketch it in the middle of the front of the notecard. Draw around the letter with other colors and widths of line. Textures may be drawn in between the

lines to add variation. (*Note:* It would be best to plan the initial design on scratch paper first, then copy it on the final notecards.)

VARIATIONS

• Draw the initial designs on one piece of paper and glue them to colored, folded cards, leaving a spacious border.
• Use the person's entire name as a basis for the design instead of the first letter of the name.

Calendar

It takes time—but a labor of love is worth all that time! This can be a lesson worked on over a period of weeks, or done in one or two art lessons. It's good practice in writing numbers, too.

MATERIALS

—white construction paper (9″ x 12″) with lines run off on a duplicating machine if possible. Twelve sheets per student.
—thin-lined felt pens, pencil and crayons, or colored pencils
—paper punch and two pieces of yarn or two brads
—construction paper to be folded over calendar for a cover (10″ x 19″)

PROCEDURE

1. Students are given twelve sheets of construction paper which have been divided into at least 31 squares with a margin at the top. Write one of the twelve months on each of the papers. Write the days of the week at the top of the squares.

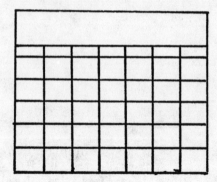

2. Teacher copies the way the following year's calendar is organized on the chalkboard and students copy this on their own calendars.

3. Discuss occasions and holidays of the year such as: Halloween, Thanksgiving, Independence Day, April Fool's Day, Valentine's Day, Groundhog Day, Columbus Day, First Day of Spring, Mother's Day, and Father's Day. Family members' birthdays may also be marked on the calendar. Draw a design or picture in the appropriate square on the calendar for each special date.

4. Draw a design on the cover paper. Punch two holes at the top of the calendar and tie all the pages together with yarn, or use brads.

VARIATIONS

• Make the calendars much smaller (such as 4″ x 5″) and make the cover out of cardboard and tissue paper as described in the *Oriental Scrapbook* gift idea on page 168.

Printed Notecards

Cardboard printing is a good beginning lesson in print making and suitable for any age. If time and care is taken in making the design, the end result is sure to be lovely.

MATERIALS

—construction paper in various colors (5″ x 4″ folded cards are a good size)
—envelopes to fit the cards can be purchased at any stationery store, if desired
—cardboard, 5″ x 4″
—tagboard or other fairly thick type of paper that students can cut
—pencil
—glue
—brayer or roller and water-soluble printing ink (*Note:* Thick tempera paint may be substituted for the printing ink.)
—inking plate, such as a piece of glass, masonite, or formica
—newspaper to work on

PROCEDURE

1. Plan the design for the print, remembering to keep it simple. Separate the various parts of the design as shown.

2. Draw these parts on the tagboard or other heavy paper and cut out each piece.

3. Put the design "back together" on the piece of cardboard, leaving a small amount of space between each section of the design. Glue each piece carefully to the cardboard. Pieces, such as eyes, may be glued on top of each other. Allow the glued design to dry thoroughly and securely by placing it under several heavy books.

4. Roll out about a tablespoon of printing ink on the inking plate with the brayer. Roll the ink carefully over the design. (*Note:* Some of the ink may get on the cardboard background and show up on the print, but it will not affect the design.) Be certain all areas of the raised tagboard design are covered with ink.

5. Press the front side of the notecard over the inked design and rub the back of the card thoroughly so that the ink comes off of the cardboard design and onto the notecard. Carefully remove the notecard from the cardboard design. Allow to dry.

6. Make as many prints as desired in this way.

7. See the ideas for packaging notecards in the *Felt Pen Notecards* idea on page 172.

VARIATIONS

• Make all the prints on one piece of paper and later cut them out and glue them onto colored pieces of folded paper.

• Use the tagboard design to make a crayon rub. Place a piece of paper over the cardboard with raised tagboard design. Rub the sides of crayons over it, until the design appears on the paper. Use several different colors of crayon. These rubbings could be substituted for the printed cards if all of the printing materials are not available.

VI–Gift Ornaments

Felt Love Dove
Dough People
Yarn Ornament
Star Santa
Paper Angel
String Star
Papier Mache Ball
20-Piece Ornament*
Hanging Bird
Papier Mache Egg
Box Animal Ornament*
Dreidel
Mistletoe Holder*
Scandinavian Heart Ornament

* More Difficult—for third grade and above

Felt Love Dove

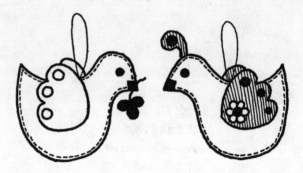

These felt birds make lovely tree ornaments, spring decorations, room decorations, mobiles, or sachets (by filling them with dried rose petals or sachet powder).

MATERIALS

—paper pattern of bird shape and straight pin to hold it
—different colors of felt
—cotton balls (four per bird)
—needle and thread
—black sequins (two per bird), ¼" diameter
—glue
—scissors (good ones for cutting felt)
—paper pattern of wing
—toothpick (for gluing)

PROCEDURE

1. Trace around a paper pattern of bird pinned to a folded piece of felt.

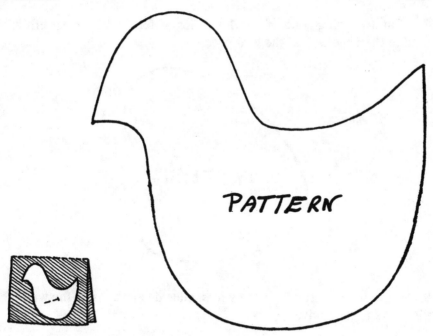

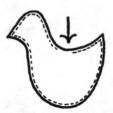

2.   Cut out the bird shape.
3.   Sew the two bird shapes together (1/8-inch from edge), leaving a 1-inch opening at top of bird for stuffing.

4.   Stuff the bird with four cotton balls (pulled apart). Use a pencil to help distribute the cotton evenly.

5.   Cut out two triangles for beak.
6.   Glue sequins (eyes) and beaks on each side of the bird's head, using a toothpick dipped in a very small amount of glue.

7.   Cut two wings out of another color of felt. A paper pattern can be used in the same way as the bird pattern.

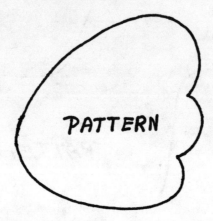

8.   Cut out decorations for the wings. Glue decorations to the wings; glue the wings to the body.

9.   Tail feathers and head decorations can be added.

10. To hang bird: Sew a thread through the top of the bird and tie it off, making a 4-inch loop. This will also close off the opening left for stuffing. Make sure that this loop is placed in a spot which balances the bird.

VARIATIONS

• Make other animals or objects using the same principle.

- Use printed fabric for the body and decorate with felt.
- Use heavy paper instead of felt.
- Make several smaller birds and hang with a larger one to make a mobile.

Dough People

This dough is pure pleasure for children to work with, and the "characters" they create with it are absolutely precious. Dough people make adorable gifts to hang on a kitchen wall, or as tree ornaments.

MATERIALS

—dough: This is the recipe for making about fourteen 4½" people:

  6 cups flour
  1 3/4 cups salt
  2 cups water (possibly a little more)
  Combine flour and salt; mix in water. KNEAD until smooth and elastic and free from lumps and dry spots.

—flour-and-water paste, or water
—tin foil or waxed paper to work on
—knife (a plastic one will do)
—toothpick
—garlic press or strainer
—shortening for browning the dough person
—wire or hairpin for hanging
—oven for baking the dough person
—Polymer medium and brush for shining the dough person

PROCEDURE

1.   Give each child a ball of dough about 2″ in diameter, a piece of tin foil or waxed paper to work on, and a spoonful of flour-and-water paste, or small amount of water. (*Note:* If the air is very dry, a damp paper towel to wrap the dough in when not working with it will keep the dough moist.)

2.   Encourage children to play with the dough to see how it works. Demonstrate one way to make a dough person.

3.   Form a ball for the head.

4.   Make a short cylinder shape for the neck.

5.   Make a longer oval for the body.

6.   Roll a "snake" for the arms and legs.

7.   Cut this "snake" into four pieces.

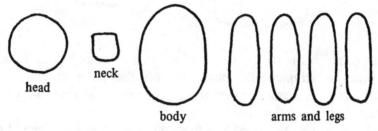

8.   Stick the person together, using flour-and-water paste, or a drop of water.

9.   Arrange the arms and legs.

10. Form a tiny ball for the nose and attach it to head.

11. Form two more tiny balls, flatten them, and attach to the face for cheeks.

12. Make two holes with a toothpick for the eyes; draw on a mouth.

13. Add clothes: Flatten out some of the dough with the palm of the hand. Using a knife, cut out skirt, pants, belt, suspenders, etc. Fold around the body and paste down the edges.

14. Add hair: This is the best part of all! Place a small ball of dough in a garlic press or strainer and push through the holes to make wavy, spaghetti-like hair. Remove from the garlic press or strainer with a knife and attach to parts of the head.

15. Add accessories that make each dough person unique (ears, fingers, shoes, hats, purses, and so forth). It is fun to have a dough person holding a bouquet of dough flowers.

16. Cloves or currants can be pushed into the eyes for an added effect. Raisins can be glued on (after baking the dough) for buttons. Sugar cookie colored decorations can be sprinkled on after the Polymer medium has been applied.

17. To hang the dough person: Attach a hairpin or wire loop to the back of the head before baking.

18. To bake: Place on a cookie sheet in a 250° oven for at least two hours. To turn golden: Rub with shortening and return to a very hot oven for a minute or two, watching carefully so that no part of the dough person gets too browned.

19. Paint the front side with Polymer medium and allow to dry.

VARIATIONS

• Don't rub shortening on the dough person, but instead paint. Shine with Polymer medium.

• Glue the dough person to a sanded, stained piece of wood and attach a hanging ring to the top of the wood.

• Make other ornaments, such as animals or heart-shaped "cookies."

yarn Ornament

A yarn ornament is attractive on a tree or wall and is extremely simple to make. The materials required can be brought from home.

MATERIALS

—tagboard or cardboard (5″ square per ornament)
—scissors
—pencil
—glue
—yarn (a variety of colors and preferably only thick yarns)
—paper towel to work on
—string to make loop (6″ per ornament)

PROCEDURE

1. Draw a pencil dot in the center of the tagboard square. (*Note:* Teacher may want to do this for the very young students.)

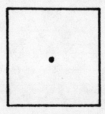

2. Practice placing the yarn on the tagboard, beginning at the dot and winding out from it. See what colors of yarn look the most interesting together. When a satisfying design has been made, cut the yarn the correct lengths.

3. Apply glue to the tagboard square, beginning at the dot. Press the yarn to the tagboard. Wind the yarn around until the edge of the tagboard is reached.

4. Cut out the circular shape.

5. Glue or tape a loop to the back of this ornament for hanging.

6. Repeat the process of gluing yarn to the back side of the ornament, so both sides of the tagboard will be completely covered with yarn.

VARIATIONS

- Draw a shape, such as a star or flower, and fill it in with yarn.

Star Santa

Star Santas can be hung from the ceiling, on the Christmas tree, on the front door or anywhere else that suits them.

MATERIALS

—star pattern
—cardboard (just large enough to fit the pattern)
—newsprint or other thin paper (12" x 18" per Santa)
—liquid starch and container to hold it
—red tissue paper (about 9" x 12" sheet per Santa)
—scissors
—paper towel or newspaper to work on
—two cotton balls per Santa
—two small black sequins per Santa
—black construction paper (4" x 2" per Santa)
—orange construction paper (1" x 1" per Santa)
—gold paper (A small piece will be enough for an entire class, as it is only
    for the belt buckle. Gold paper is often found on Christmas cards.)
—glue
—Polymer medium, P.V.A., or wallpaper glaze to shine Santa (optional)
—string to hang Santa
—tin foil to dry stars on

PROCEDURE

1.   Trace star shape onto cardboard.

PATTERN

2.   Cut out star shape.

3.   Tear up a sheet of newsprint or thin paper into small pieces, cover with liquid starch, and put on the star. Apply to both sides, making sure to cover all the edges.

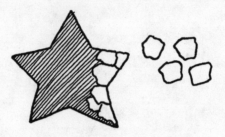

4.   Apply a final layer of red tissue paper, torn into pieces, with the starch. Make sure all the edges are covered.

5.   Allow to dry completely. Dry on tin foil and turn over when the top is dry so the bottom will dry.

6.   Cut out two sets of the following: belt and black boots, green mittens. Cut out two orange circles for cheeks and a smaller orange circle for a nose. Glue these on the star. (*Note:* One entire point of the star will be Santa's cap. The face is below this.)

7.   Add cotton for: the beard, tassel on the hat, and trim around the hat, and cuffs.

8.   Paint the entire star with Polymer medium, P.V.A., or wallpaper glaze to shine it (optional).

9.   Add two sequins for the eyes.

10.   Attach a loop of string at the top of the hat. It can be glued under the cotton tassel.

VARIATIONS

- Make an elf or some other creature using the same technique.
- Use felt instead of the cardboard, newsprint, and tissue paper.
- Paint the newsprint-covered star instead of applying tissue paper, although tissue paper collage over newsprint papier mache makes the effect smoother.

Paper Angel

Lovely, crisp-looking, white angel decorations would look beautiful almost anywhere. They are a one-session project.

MATERIALS

—white paper, two 9" x 5" sheets per angel
—gold paper (2½" x 2½" sheet)
—glue
—scissors
—thin toothpick
—½" diameter styrofoam ball or ½" diameter paper circle
—cotton ball for hair
—paper towel to work on
—thin-lined felt pens or colored pencils
—needle and thread to make loop for hanging

PROCEDURE

1. Fold the two 9" x 5" sheets of white paper accordian-style, making ½" folds.
2. Bend the two folded pieces 1½" from top.

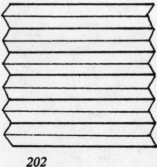

3. Put eyes, nose, mouth, and cheeks on the styrofoam ball or paper circle. Glue cotton on the top for hair.

4. Glue the two folded pieces of white paper together, leaving the 1½″ at the top unglued.

5. Stick a thin toothpick into the styrofoam ball (or glue toothpick to the back of the paper face) and stick the other end of the toothpick down into the glued part of the folded paper.

6. Add wings and halo by gluing the gold paper to the back of the angel. Use the pattern shown for the wings and halo or create a new one.

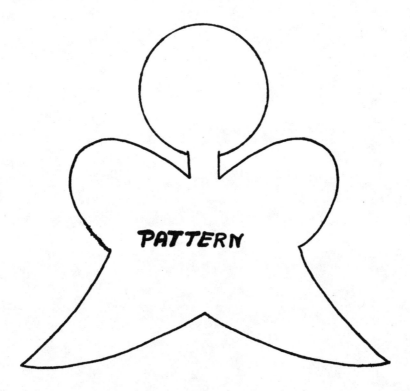

PATTERN

7. Sew thread through the top of the halo for a hanger.

VARIATIONS

• Make three angels and stick them into a styrofoam block with cotton around them to look like a cloud.
• Make three or more angels and hang as a mobile, using directions for making a mobile on page 60.

String Star

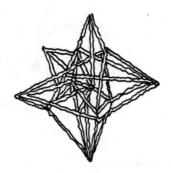

This is a quick-to-make idea and very pretty, particularly when hanging on a green tree.

MATERIALS

—cardboard (about 6" x 6")
—straight pins (about one dozen per star)
—liquid starch or half water-half white glue mixture
—brush (or finger)
—any color of string or thin yarn
—glitter (optional)

PROCEDURE

1. Stick the straight pins into the cardboard at varying distances apart so as to form the general pattern of a star.

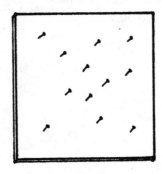

2. Loop string around the pins to form geometric shapes.

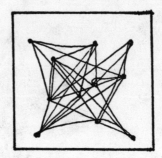

3. When a form develops that is interesting and not too sparse of string, brush liquid starch onto the entire string surface very thoroughly. Glitter may be sprinkled on at this time.

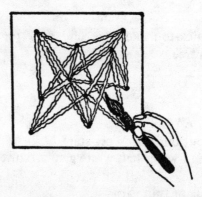

4. Allow to dry. When completely dry and stiff, remove the pins from the cardboard and star.

VARIATIONS

• Make four or more small stars and make a mobile. (Follow directions for making a mobile on page 60.)

Papier Mache Ball

This is a several step project, but a good papier mache lesson.

MATERIALS

—newspaper to work on
—newspaper to wad into ball. One full sheet makes about a 3″ diameter ball.
—masking tape or cellophane tape to hold wadded ball together
—tissue paper (various colors)
—liquid starch and container for it (wheat paste may be substituted)
—newsprint strips (approximately 3/4″ x 12″)
—Polymer medium, P.V.A., or wallpaper glaze to be brushed on, or spray lacquer
—glitter to sprinkle on at the end (optional)
—for hanger (one suggestion): small circle of felt, staple, and 4″ piece of thin wire.

PROCEDURE

1. Wad newspaper into as round a ball as possible. Hold it together with two or three pieces of masking tape. (*Note:* Tape can be distributed to everyone by having a student or students stick two or three 3″ strips on the edge of the table or desk where each child is working.)

2. Each child should have in front of him: newspaper to work on, the newspaper "ball," liquid starch in a container, and a dozen or more 3/4″ x 12″ newsprint or other thin paper strips. Dip the strips into liquid starch, soak them thoroughly and wrap them around the newspaper "ball." Apply the strips in all directions. Tell students to "hug" and "pet" the ball often as they work. Shape the ball as the strips are added. Make sure that all of the newspaper is covered by the strips. Smooth all edges down by rubbing starch over the entire ball.

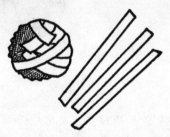

3. Add the tissue paper. This may be added before the strips have dried. Tear different shapes of tissue paper into uneven pieces (approximately 1½″ squares). Overlap the pieces of tissue paper until the entire ball is covered. Use starch to stick the tissue paper pieces to the ball, and rub starch over the entire ball to smooth down the tissue paper. (*Note:* There are good color combinations to use on the balls, such as: blue, green, and lavender; orange, red, and hot pink; green, yellow, and turquoise.)

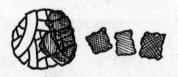

4. Allow the ball to dry. Place on waxed paper or tin foil so the ball will not stick. Turn occasionally so the area underneath can dry. (*Note:* Write each child's name in a place on the drying area so it will be known to whom each ornament belongs.)
5. Attach hanger: Put a staple through a small round piece of felt. Choose a color of felt that blends with the tissue paper on the ball and glue the felt circle on the ball. Slip a thin piece of wire under the staple and make a 2-inch loop.
6. Paint the ornament with Polymer medium, P.V.A., or wallpaper glaze, or spray lacquer by holding onto the hanger with one hand. Hang the ornament up to dry. (*Note:* A clothesline can be hung in the room and the ornaments can be hung with paper clips or masking tape.)

VARIATIONS

- Sprinkle glitter on the ball after the final shiny coat has been added.
- Cut designs out of the tissue paper and stick to the ball over the papier mache.
- Using the same technique, make a piece of fruit (such as an apple or pear) and attach green felt leaves to the top.

20 Piece Ornament

Here is one of the most fascinating to make of all the gift ideas. It delights children of all ages (adults too!)

MATERIALS

—construction paper or any type of paper.
—scissors
—pencil
—circle pattern (2½" in diameter)
—triangle pattern and tagboard to trace it onto.
—glue, or stapler and thirty staples per ornament
—ribbon or piece of yarn

PROCEDURE

1. Trace twenty circles on colored paper. One color, several colors, or many colors will do.

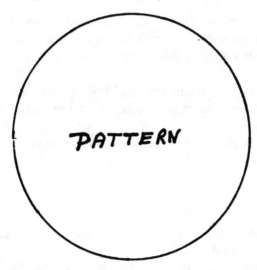

2. Cut them out.
3. Fold all twenty circles over a triangle shape cut out of tagboard.

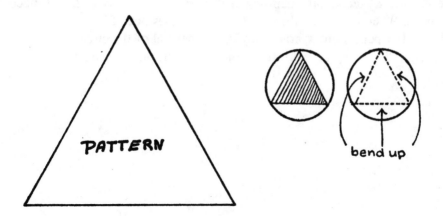

bend up

4. Begin to "build" the ball: Staple or glue the first five circles together with the points of the triangles down to form the base of the ball.

5. Then add a row of ten circles, five with bases stapled or glued to the base of the first five, and the others between them with points down. All sides that are touching other sides should be secured with staples, or flaps glued down.

6. To round out the top of the ball, add the last five circles by stapling or gluing them with their bases to the bases of the last circles added, and then to each other.

7. After the ball is all together, attach a ribbon or piece of yarn. Glue it between one of the flaps.

VARIATIONS

• A pinking shears, instead of scissors, may be used to cut out the twenty circles, for a different effect.

• Any size ornament can be made by changing the size of the twenty circles.

• With water colors, paint a sheet of 12" x 18" drawing paper, using a "wet-into-wet" technique (painting with very wet paint onto a wet piece of paper). When this paper dries, cut twenty circles out of it.

• With a felt pen, write words or sayings on several of the circles.

• Glue smaller triangles, cut out of colored paper, on the ornament.

Hanging Bird

This is a good gift idea for the very young child. Hanging birds are very colorful, and several different-colored birds are simply lovely when displayed together.

MATERIALS

—bird shape pattern (or let children draw their own)
—construction paper (6″ x 4″ per bird) in various colors
—pencil
—scissors
—paper punch
—colored tissue paper (6″ by 9″ per bird)
—needle and thread for hanging bird
—felt pens for decorating bird (optional)

PROCEDURE

1. Trace the bird shape on the colored construction paper.

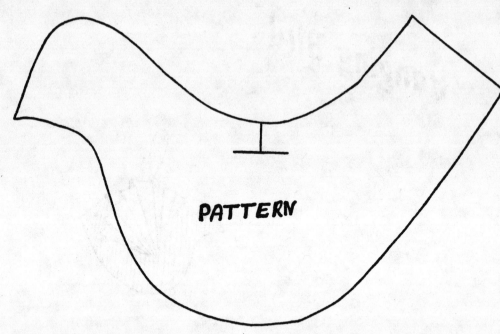

PATTERN

2. Cut out the bird and cut the paper along the "T." This is where the wings will later be inserted.

3. Use the paper punch to make an eye and a design in the tail. Or, use felt pens to make the eye and tail decorations.

4. Fold the tissue paper accordian-style in 5/8" folds.

5. Slip this folded piece of tissue paper through the slit in the bird, half way.

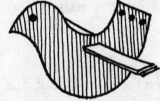

6. Spread out the folds to form a fan. Fasten the two ends that come together with the needle and thread. Make a loop of thread to hang the bird at the same time.

VARIATIONS

• Make the bird's body with the papier mache technique as explained in the *Star Santa Ornament* idea on page 198.

• Use colored cardboard to make the body, and construction or origami paper to make the wings.

Papier Mache Egg

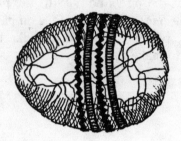

This pleasant-looking object is an excellent lesson in papier mache and lots of fun for any aged student.

MATERIALS

—balloon
—strips of newsprint (3/4" x 12"), several dozen per egg
—liquid starch (or wheat paste) and container
—tin foil, waxed paper, plastic, or oil cloth to dry eggs on
—tissue paper, different colors
—rickrack, trim, ribbon or strips of colored paper
—glue
—Polymer medium, P.V.A., or wallpaper glaze to shine the eggs

PROCEDURE

1. Blow up small balloons and tie off. (*Note:* It will save time if the balloons are blown up and tied before given to a class.)
2. Apply the newsprint strips after they have been soaked thoroughly with liquid starch or wheat paste. It may be difficult to get the first few strips to stick to the balloon, but after four or five strips are crisscrossed on each other, the rest stick easily. Cover the entire balloon with strips,

smoothing them down carefully so there are no edges sticking up. Apply the strips as close to the balloon's knot as possible.

3. Allow the egg to dry, which will make a hard shell around the balloon. At this time, cut off the knot of the balloon. Have each child write his name in pencil on the egg.

4. Tear tissue paper into uneven pieces and apply to the egg with liquid starch. A brush or fingers can be used to apply the liquid starch (but the fingers will become temporarily colored!). Cover the entire egg with tissue paper, overlapping the pieces. Put several layers over the hole where the knot of the balloon had been. (Good color combinations are: blue, green, and lavender; orange, red, and hot pink; green, yellow, and turquoise.)

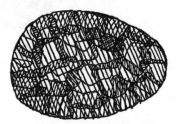

5. Place on tin foil, waxed paper, oil cloth, or plastic to dry, and turn occasionally. (*Note:* Write each child's name in a place on the drying area so it will be known to whom each egg belongs.)

6. Shine the egg by painting on Polymer medium, P.V.A., or wallpaper glaze, holding the balloon carefully with two fingers. Allow to dry.

7. To decorate the colored egg further, glue rickrack, ribbon, trim, or strips of colored paper around the egg. (*Note:* An effective way to gift wrap the egg is in a shoe box with green paper grass around it. This "grass" can be made by cutting tissue paper or construction paper on the paper cutter.)

VARIATIONS

• When the egg shell is hard, it can be sliced in two with a matt knife and a "surprise" can be placed inside.

• Cut designs out of the tissue paper and apply them to the egg instead of the torn tissue paper pieces.

Box
Animal
Ornament

Making Box Animals is one of the longer projects shown in this book, but the results are well worth the time and effort involved. They are absolutely adorable!

MATERIALS

—Tagboard to make the 2″ square box (two strips, 2″ x 10″)
—masking tape to tape box
—newsprint strips (at least four strips, 2″ x 10″)
—liquid starch or wheat paste and container
—newspaper to work on
—Polymer medium, P.V.A., or wallpaper glaze and brush to shine box
    (optional)
—tin foil, waxed paper, oil cloth, or plastic to dry cube on
—pieces of felt for animal's features
—yarn, ribbon, feathers, cotton, sequins, buttons, rickrack, and other
    items to decorate the box

PROCEDURE

1. Bend the two tagboard strips four times each, making five 2″ squares.

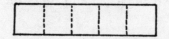

2. Fold the first strip into a box and tape last fold down.

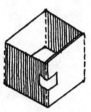

3. Fold the second strip the same way and bend around the other folded and taped strip, making a hollow cube. Tape this down also.

4. Apply the newsprint strips to the cube with liquid starch or wheat paste. Wrap these strips around the cube carefully, following the sides of the cube. When these strips have dried, the cube should be quite sturdy.

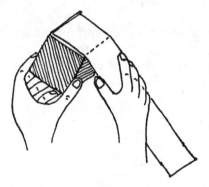

5. Apply torn pieces of tissue paper to the cube. Make certain that all edges are covered and the tissue paper has been smoothed down. Place on tin foil, waxed paper, oil cloth, or plastic to dry.

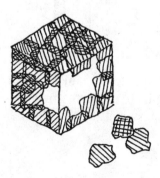

6. Shine the cube by brushing on Polymer medium, P.V.A., or wallpaper glaze and allow to dry.

7. Add features cut from felt and other items listed in *Materials*.

8. To hang the box animal ornament: Sew a thread loop through a small piece of felt and glue to the top of the box. Or, put a staple through the piece of felt, slip a thin piece of wire under the staple and form a loop; glue the felt to the top of the box.

VARIATIONS

• Make the cubes into small packages.

• Use individual cereal boxes (rectangular shaped) or other small boxes to make this project. This will eliminate the first few steps.
• Print words on the cube, such as JOY, LOVE, PEACE, HOPE.

Dreidel

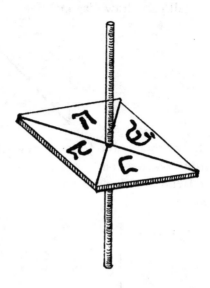

Jewish children are familiar with this little top, but it would be fun to let everyone know about it.

MATERIALS

—2″ square cardboard
—cotton swab (minus the cotton) or other stick
—felt pens
—glue
—large needle to put hole in center of the cardboard
—ruler or straight piece of cardboard to draw lines

PROCEDURE

1. Before beginning the project, explain what a dreidle is. It is a top with four Hebrew letters on it, which also have number values. "Put and Take" games are played with the dreidle using these numbers. The four Hebrew letters are Nun נ, Gimel ג, Hay ה, and Shin שׁ. They stand for "a great miracle happened there," which refers to the oil that was used to light the menorah (the Jewish holy candelabra). This oil lasted for eight days. How to play the game: Each player in turn spins the dreidle and wins the number of points corresponding to the Hebrew letter which stands upright when the dreidle has stopped spinning. The number of the Hebrew letters: נ = 50, ג = 3, ה = 5, שׁ = 300.

2. With a felt pen, draw diagonal lines on the square of cardboard.

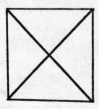

3. Carefully draw in the four Hebrew letters and go over them with a felt pen. (*Note:* Teacher may want to draw a large square on the chalkboard with the Hebrew letters shown and the order in which they are placed on the dreidle.)

4. The cardboard square may be decorated with colored felt pens (or crayons).

5. Jab the needle into the center of the square to make a hole for the swab stick. Be sure the cotton on the end of the stick has been removed. (*Note:* It is possible to purchase thin, round sticks without the cotton tips at some drug stores.) Insert the swab stick through the hole, half way. Brush a drop of glue over the hole to hold the stick in place. It is important to make sure the stick is perpendicular to the cardboard.

VARIATIONS

• Thin plywood and dowels could be substituted for the cardboard and cotton swab sticks. The children could sand the edges with sandpaper and shellac the finished dreidle. A drill would be required for making the hole.

Mistletoe Holder

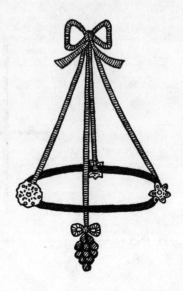

This is a cute idea for a gift, particularly if a member of the class has access to mistletoe. If it isn't available, ideas found in the *Variations* section can easily be substituted.

MATERIALS

—a 24" x 1" strip of cardboard or tagboard (red, white, or green is ideal)
—glue or staple
—five pieces of red yarn or ribbon, 18" long each (or 7½ feet)
—mistletoe (or substitute)
—white paper for making snowflakes (3" x 3" squares, three each)
—scissors

PROCEDURE

1. Bend cardboard strip into a circle, overlap ends about one inch, and glue or staple.

2. At three evenly spaced points on the hoop, tie one end of three of the 18" red ribbons or yarn.

3. Gather the tops of these three ribbons and adjust ends until the hoop hangs evenly.

4. Slip one end of another 18″ ribbon among these ends, so that this ribbon hangs down in the center of the hoop. Holding the four top ends firmly, staple together (or wrap with string).

5. Tie the last 18″ ribbon over the ends. Make a bow.

6. Make three small, dainty snowflakes to place on the hoop at the three spots where the ribbon has been tied. Here are directions for making simple snowflakes:

    a)   Fold paper square in half, then into fourths. For the third and last fold, fold this diagonally in half, making a triangle.

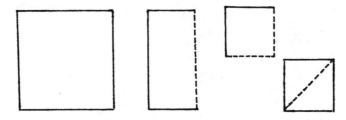

    b)   Cut out shapes along the three sides of the triangle. Remember not to cut clear through or across the triangle, or the snowflake will fall apart.

    c)   Open up the paper and see how the snowflake looks. If not satisfied with it, fold the paper again and make further cuts on it.

(*Note:* It may be a good idea to have the children practice cutting a snowflake a few times before they make the final ones for their mistletoe holder.)

7. Glue or staple these snowflakes over the three knots on the hoop.

8. Tie the ribbon hanging in the middle of the hoop to a piece of mistletoe.

9. Hang on the ceiling with a thumbtack or piece of tape.

VARIATIONS

• Substitute a felt love dove for the mistletoe. Directions are given on page 188.

• Wrap the hoop with a red or green crepe paper strip (approximately 1″ by 1 yd.).

• Substitute other items, such as paper sculpture candles, birds, or ribbon bows, for the snowflakes.

• Make six or more snowflakes to glue on the hoop.

Scandinavian Heart Ornament

A simple Scandinavian ornament is fun to make and lovely to see hanging on a tree, in a window, or in a doorway.

MATERIALS

—construction paper or heavier paper, 5" x 4" piece if ornament is to be all one color
—green construction paper, 1" square will be plenty
—glue
—scissors
—paper to work on
—thread
—toothpick to glue with

PROCEDURE

1. Cut out six identical hearts.

PATTERN

2. Fold each one in half carefully.

3. Place a small amount of glue on the outside center fold of one of the hearts, and stick it to the outside center fold of a second heart. Be sure to apply glue only to the fold line.

4. Place glue on the outside fold of another heart and stick it between two hearts. Glue should only be placed along the fold line.
5. Repeat step number four until all of the folded hearts have been glued to the center "core." Allow to dry.
6. Add the green trim or "leaves" by placing a dot of glue on the fold line and glue to the top of the six hearts.
7. Add thread for hanging. This can be accomplished by gluing it to "leaves," using a needle to sew it through bottom of "leaves," or bringing it from bottom of hearts and tying it at the top. Make a 2-inch loop for hanging.

VARIATIONS

• Make the hearts out of three different colors of paper, such as red, orange, and hot pink.
• Make the ornament fuller by using twelve hearts instead of six.
• Make one large heart ornament and several small ones, and hang small ones from larger ornament to make a mobile.